GRADED GO PROBLEMS
FOR BEGINNERS

VOLUME TWO
ELEMENTARY PROBLEMS

by

Kano Yoshinori 9-dan

The Nihon Ki-in

Published by
The Nihon Ki-in
7-2 Gobancho,
Chiyoda-ku, Tokyo,
Japan

First Printing September 1985
Printed in Japan
by
Sokosha Printing Co., Ltd.
Typeset on an IBM Electronic Composer
by The Ishi Press, Inc.

TABLE OF CONTENTS

PREFACE

This volume is a continuation of the first volume of GRADED GO PROBLEMS FOR BEGINNERS and is aimed at the 20-kyu to 25-kyu player.

The problems presented here will require a bit of thought, but none of them is so difficult that a player who understands the rules and has studied the first volume wouldn't be able to solve them in less than a minute.

Since the main aim of this series is to present as many examples of go technique as possible, I have avoided giving a lot of different variations of possible answers. The reader is advised to attempt to 'refute' the correct answer until he knows beyond doubt that the correct answer works. By pondering each problem in this way, the reader will develop an instinct for finding the winning move in his games.

September, 1985   Kano Yoshinori 9-dan

GLOSSARY

atari — check, i.e. a move threatening to capture on the next move.

dame — neutral points which profit neither Black nor White.

dan — a rank given to players to indicate their strength at the game. When a player's strength improves after attaining the rank of 1-kyu, he is promoted to amateur 1-dan and as he becomes stronger, the numerical value of his *dan* increases. The top amateur dan rank is usually 6-dan. The professional dan ranks start at 1-dan and go up to 9-dan, which is the highest rank attainable. A professional 1-dan is usually about two stones stronger than an amateur 6-dan. See *kyu*.

double atari — giving atari to two different groups of stones at the same time.

eye — a point on the board which is surrounded by stones of the same color.

ko — a shape in which your stone is captured but it is illegal to retake the capturing stones even though you can occupy all of its liberties.

kyu — a rank given to players to indicate their strength at the game. Beginners are arbitrarily classified at 30-kyu and as they become stronger, the numerical value of their *kyu* decreases. For example, 15-kyu is stronger than 20-kyu. See *dan*.

nakade — a large eye-space which, by skillful play, can be reduced to a single eye.

oiotoshi — a move which gives atari to a group of stones in such a way that no matter how one defends, the group will still be in atari.

oshitsubushi — a shape in which you give atari to two or more of your opponent's stones in such a way that he cannot defend against this atari without committing suicide.

seki — an impasse or stalemate between groups: if one side tries to attack the other side's group, his own group is put into atari and dies. Therefore, neither side can attack or attempt to atari.

snapback — a tactic in which one stone is offered as a sacrifice and if it is taken, the capturing stones are in turn captured.

PART ONE

PROBLEMS

I ELEMENTARY PROBLEMS
LEVEL ONE

SECTION 1. HOW TO CAPTURE STONES

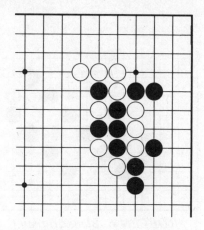

PROBLEM 1. Black to play.
How does Black play?

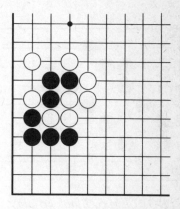

PROBLEM 2. Black to play.
How does Black play?

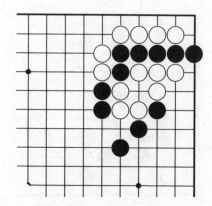

PROBLEM 3. Black to play.
How does Black play?

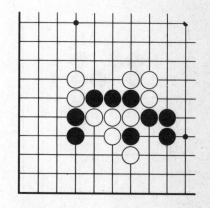

PROBLEM 4. Black to play.
How does Black play so as to
capture four white stones?

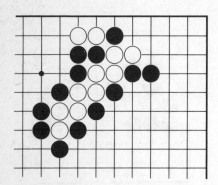

PROBLEM 5. Black to play.
How does Black play so as to
capture nine white stones?

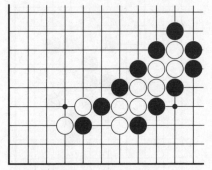

PROBLEM 6. Black to play.
How does Black play so as to
capture eight white stones?

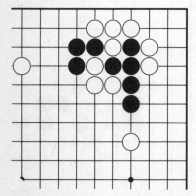

PROBLEM 7. Black to play.
How does Black play so as to
capture three white stones?

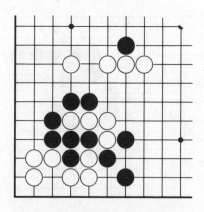

PROBLEM 8. Black to play.
How does Black play so as to
capture four white stones?

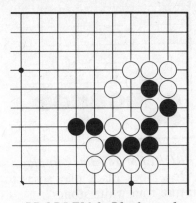

PROBLEM 9. Black to play.
How does Black play so as to connect his stones on the left and the right?

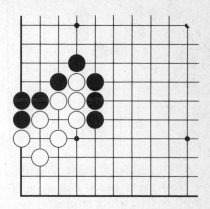

PROBLEM 10. Black to play.
How does Black play?

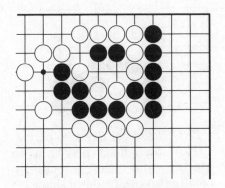

PROBLEM 11. Black to play.
How does Black play?

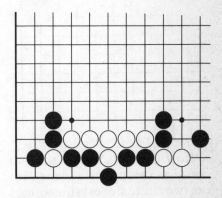

PROBLEM 12. Black to play.
How does Black play so that his stones on the edge will not be captured?

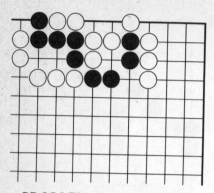

PROBLEM 13. *Black to play.*
How does Black play so as to capture five white stones?

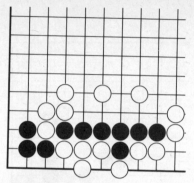

PROBLEM 14. *Black to play.*
How does Black play so as to capture four white stones?

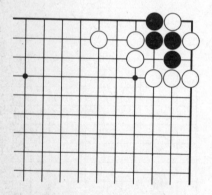

PROBLEM 15. *Black to play.*
How does Black play so as to create an oshitsubushi shape with the two white stones in the corner?

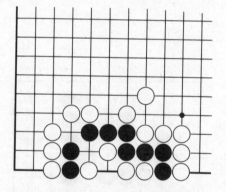

PROBLEM 16. *Black to play.*
How does Black play so as to capture four white stones by creating an oshitsubushi shape?

oshitsubushi — a shape in which you give atari to two or more of your opponent's stones in such a way that he cannot defend against this atari without committing suicide.

SECTION 2. CONNECTING AND SEPARATING STONES

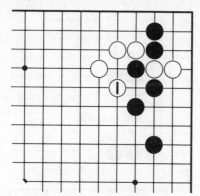

PROBLEM 17. Black to play.
How does Black play after White 1?

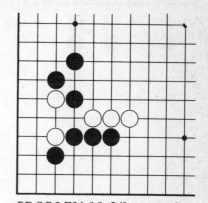

PROBLEM 18. White to play.
How does White play so as to link up all of his stones?

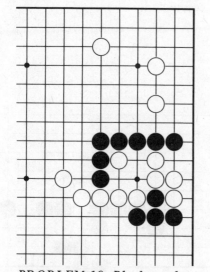

PROBLEM 19. Black to play.
How does Black play so as to separate the four white stones on the edge from those leading out into the center?

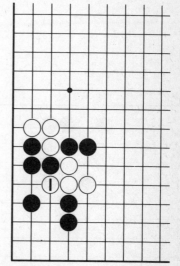

PROBLEM 20. Black to play.
How does Black play in response to White 1?

SECTION 3. DEFENDING YOUR POSITIONS

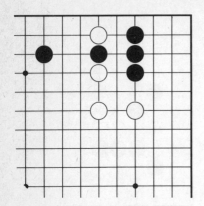

PROBLEM 21. *White to play.*
How does White give atari to the lone black stone?

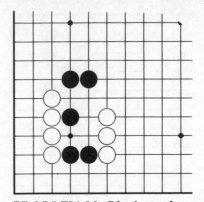

PROBLEM 22. *Black to play.*
If Black makes a "bamboo joint", all of his stones will be connected.

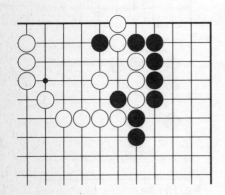

PROBLEM 23. *Black to play.*
How does Black play?

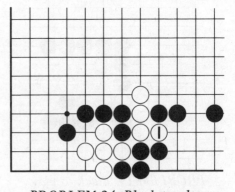

PROBLEM 24. *Black to play.*
How does Black play so that his four stones on the edge will not be captured?

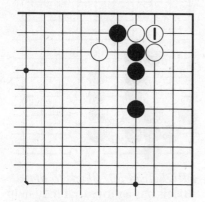

PROBLEM 25. *Black to play.*
How does Black play after White 1?

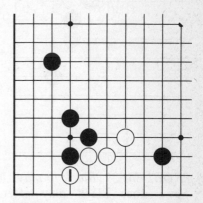

PROBLEM 26. *Black to play.*
How does Black play after White 1?

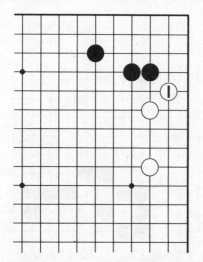

PROBLEM 27. *Black to play.*
How does Black play after White 1?

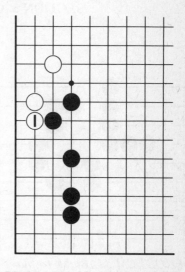

PROBLEM 28. *Black to play.*
How does Black play after White 1?

SECTION 4. KO

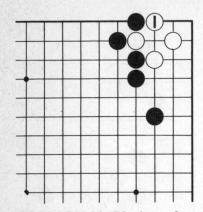

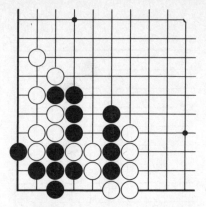

PROBLEM 29. *Black to play.*
How does Black play after White creates a ko situation with 1?

PROBLEM 30. *Black to play.*
Black has a move that may help him rescue his six stones in the corner.

SECTION 5. CAPTURING RACES

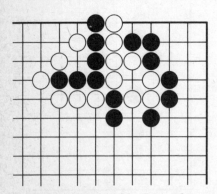

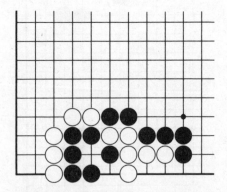

PROBLEM 31. *Black to play.*
To which group of white stones should Black give atari?

PROBLEM 32. *Black to play.*
How does Black play so as to catch the six white stones on the edge?

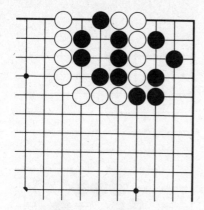

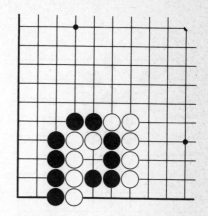

PROBLEM 33. White to play.
How does White play so as to capture the black stones on the left?

PROBLEM 34. White to play.
How does White play so as to capture four black stones?

SECTION 6. LIVING GROUPS AND DEAD GROUPS

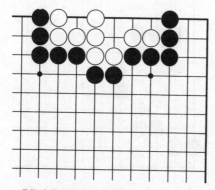

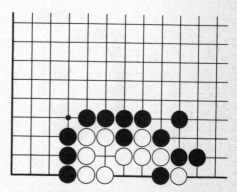

PROBLEM 35. Black to play.
How does Black play so as to kill the white stones?

PROBLEM 36. Black to play.
How does Black play so as to kill the white stones?

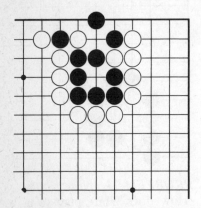

PROBLEM 37. Black to play.
How does Black play so as to give his stones life?

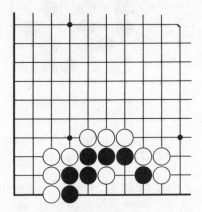

PROBLEM 38. Black to play.
How does Black play so as to give his stones life?

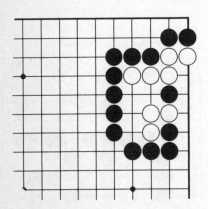

PROBLEM 39. White to play.
How does White play so as to give his stones life?

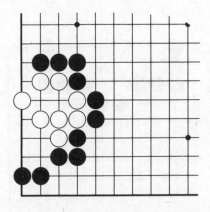

PROBLEM 40. White to play.
How does White play so as to give his stones life?

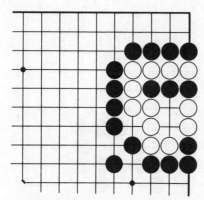

PROBLEM 41. Black to play.
How does Black play so as to
kill the white stones?

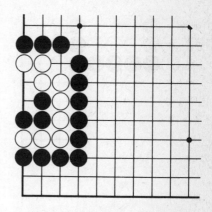

PROBLEM 42. Black to play.
How does Black play so as to
kill the white stones?

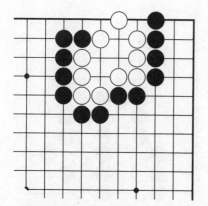

PROBLEM 43. Black to play.
How does Black play so as to
kill the white stones?

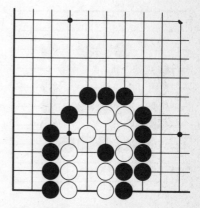

PROBLEM 44. Black to play.
How does Black play so as to
kill the white stones?

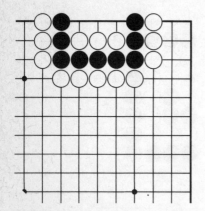

PROBLEM 45. Black to play.
How does Black play so that his stones will live in seki?

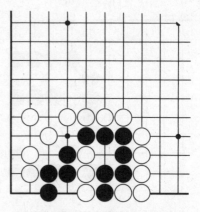

PROBLEM 46. Black to play.
How does Black play so his stones will live?

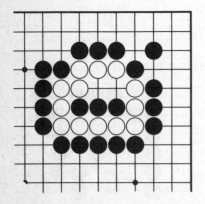

PROBLEM 47. Alive or dead?
Are the white stones alive in seki or are they dead?

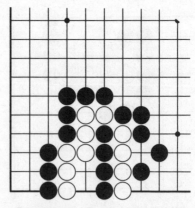

PROBLEM 48. Alive or dead?
Are the white stones alive in seki or are they dead?

— 14 —

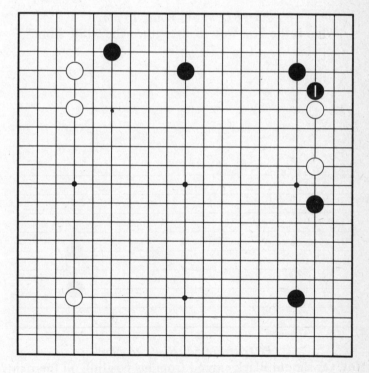

PROBLEM 49. White to play.
How should White respond to Black 1?

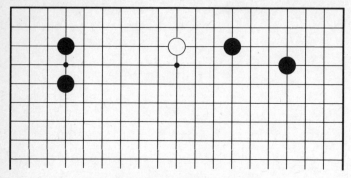

PROBLEM 50. White to play.
What is the best way to strengthen the white stone?

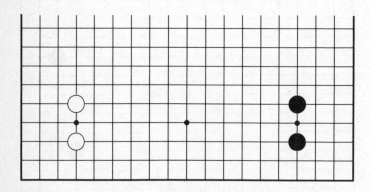

PROBLEM 51. Black to play.
How far should Black extend from his position on the right?

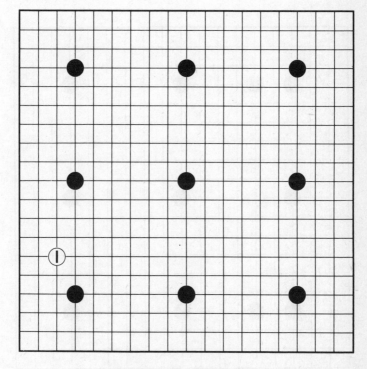

PROBLEM 52. Black to play.
How should Black play in response to White 1?
(There is more than one correct answer.)

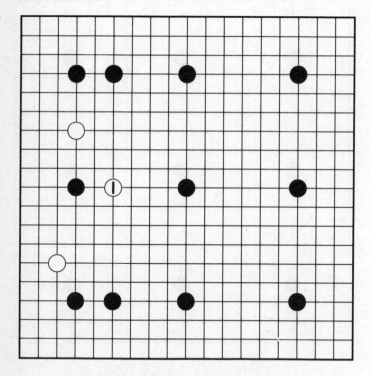

PROBLEM 53. *Black to play.*
How should Black respond to White 1?
(There is more than one correct answer.)

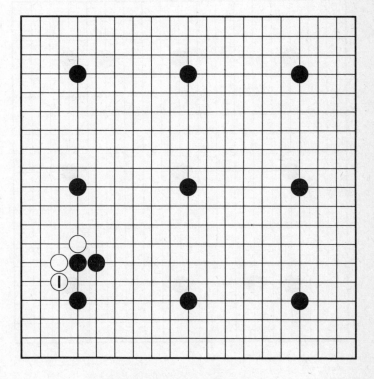

PROBLEM 54. Black to play.
How should Black play in response to White 1?

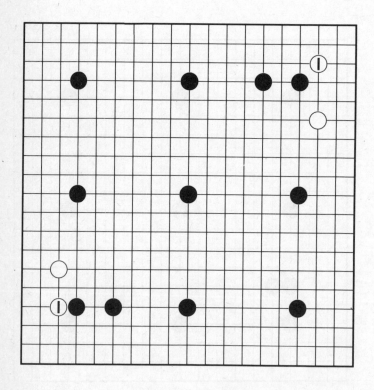

PROBLEM 55. Black to play.
How should Black respond to White 1 at the top right of the board?

PROBLEM 56. Black to play.
How should Black respond to White 1 at the bottom left of the board?

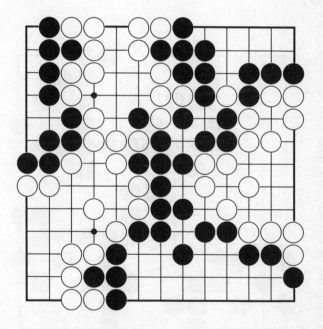

PROBLEM 57. Defects in the territories.

Both Black and White have defects in their territories and must defend these weaknesses before they can consider their territories completed.

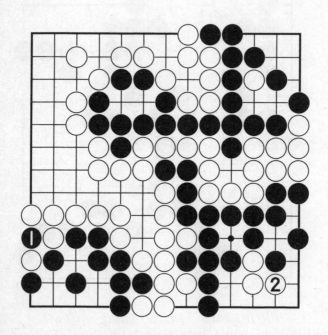

PROBLEM 58. Black to play.
In response to Black's taking a ko with 1, White has played 2. How should Black reply?

II ELEMENTARY PROBLEMS
LEVEL TWO

SECTION 1. HOW TO PLAY IN THE OPENING

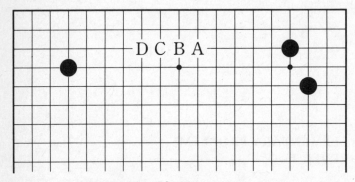

PROBLEM 59. White to play.
Which of the four points from A to D should White play?
(There is more than one correct answer.)

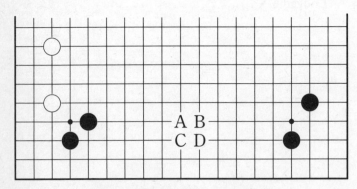

PROBLEM 60. White to play.
Which of the four points from A to D should White play?
(There is more than one correct answer.)

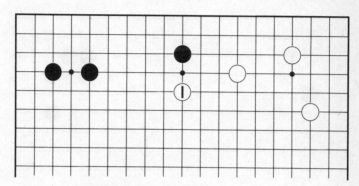

PROBLEM 61. Black to play.

White plays a capping move over a black stone with 1. How should Black respond?

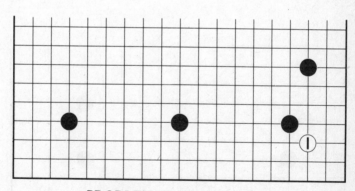

PROBLEM 62. Black to play.

White invades the corner with 1. How should Black block? From the left or from above?

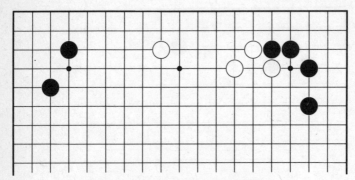

PROBLEM 63. Black to play.
Where should Black play?

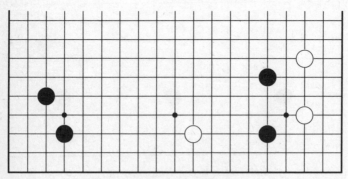

PROBLEM 64. Black to play.
Where should Black play?

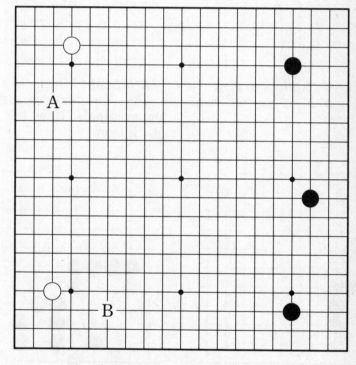

PROBLEM 65. White to play.
At which point should White make a corner enclosure, A or B?

SECTION 2. HOW TO CAPTURE STONES
AND RELATED PROBLEMS

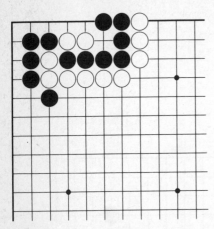

PROBLEM 66. Black to play.
  How can Black capture two white stones?

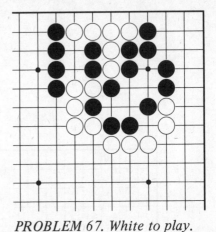

PROBLEM 67. White to play.
  The six white stones at the top are in danger. How can White rescue them?

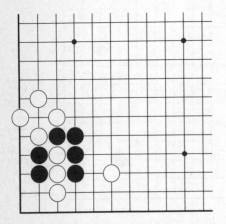

PROBLEM 68. Black to play.
  How can Black capture three white stones?

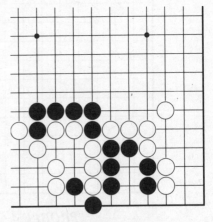

PROBLEM 69. Black to play.
  How should Black play?

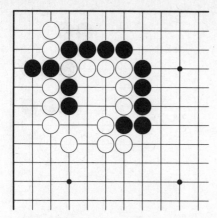

PROBLEM 70. Black to play.
How can Black capture six white stones?

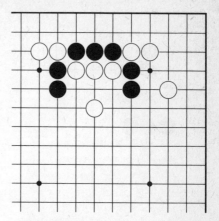

PROBLEM 71. Black to play.
How can Black capture three white stones?

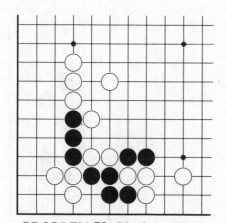

PROBLEM 72. Black to play.
How can Black capture two white stones?

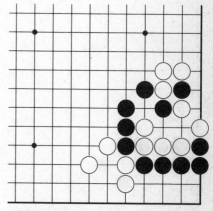

PROBLEM 73. Black to play.
How can Black capture four white stones?

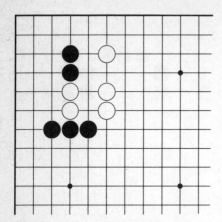

PROBLEM 74. *Black to play.*
How can Black link up his stones above to the ones below?

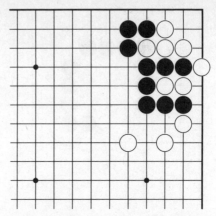

PROBLEM 75. *White to play.*
How can White link up his stones above to the ones below?

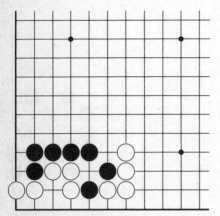

PROBLEM 76. *Black to play.*
How can Black capture the five white stones in the corner?

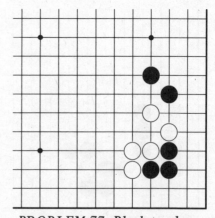

PROBLEM 77. *Black to play.*
How can Black link up his stones below to the ones above?

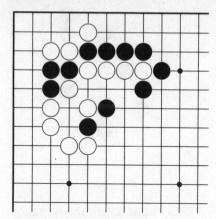

PROBLEM 78. Black to play.
How can Black capture four white stones?

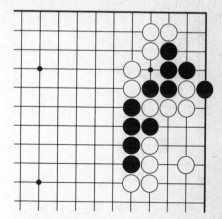

PROBLEM 79. Black to play.
How can Black capture four white stones?

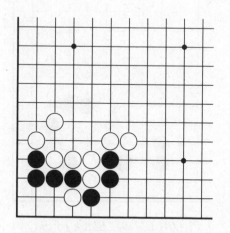

PROBLEM 80. Black to play.
How should Black play?

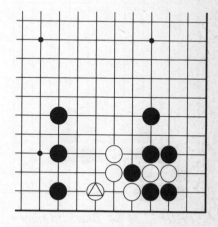

PROBLEM 81. White to play.
How should White play so as to utilize his marked stone?

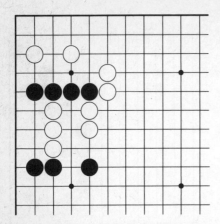

PROBLEM 82. Black to play.
How can Black link up his stones above to the ones below?

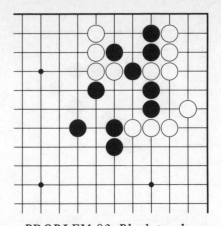

PROBLEM 83. Black to play.
How can Black link up all of his stones?

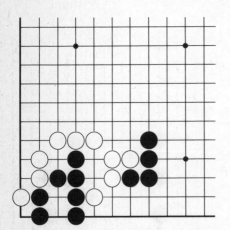

PROBLEM 84. Black to play.
How can Black link up his stones on the left to the ones on the right?

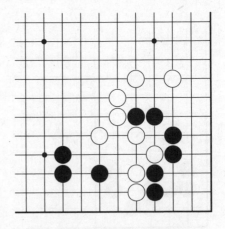

PROBLEM 85. Black to play.
Can Black separate some of the white stones near the edge from the ones in the center?

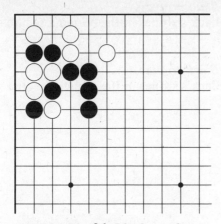

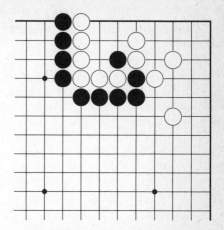

PROBLEM 86. Black to play.
How can Black capture three white stones?

PROBLEM 87. Black to play.
How can Black capture six white stones?

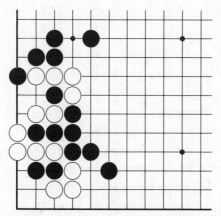

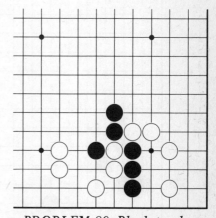

PROBLEM 88. Black to play.
How can Black capture four white stones?

PROBLEM 89. Black to play.
How can Black capture two white stones?

SECTION 3. DEFENDING YOUR POSITIONS

PROBLEM 90. Black to play.
Where is the point that will give Black's stones in the corner a secure shape?

PROBLEM 91. Black to play.
Where is the point that will give Black's stones in the corner a secure shape?

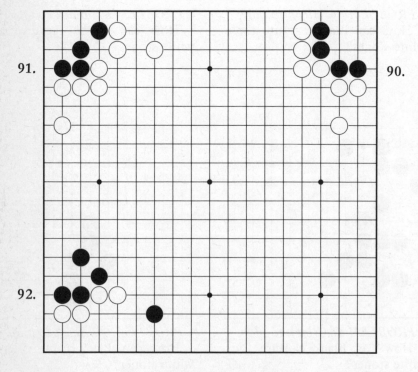

PROBLEM 92. Black to play.
Where is the point for Black to attack the four white stones?

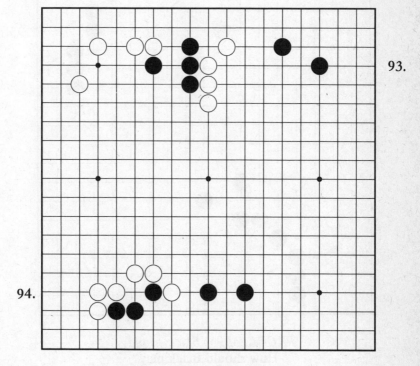

93.

94.

PROBLEM 94. Black to play.
How should Black play?

PROBLEM 95. Black to play.
How should Black play?

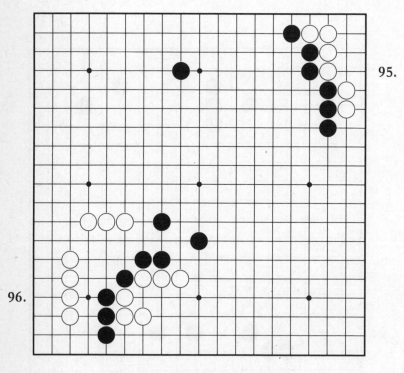

95.

96.

PROBLEM 96. Black to play.
How should Black play?

PROBLEM 97. Black to play.

How should Black play? Also, if it were White's turn, how would he play?

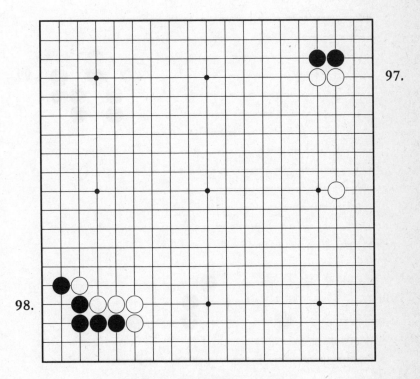

97.

98.

PROBLEM 98. White to play.
How should White play?

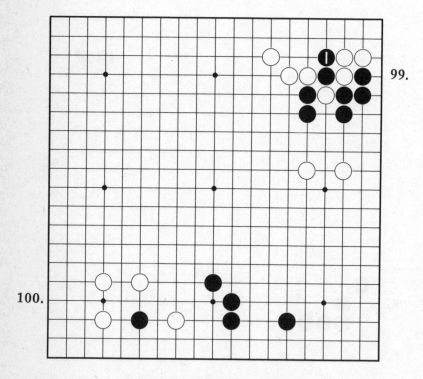

99.

100.

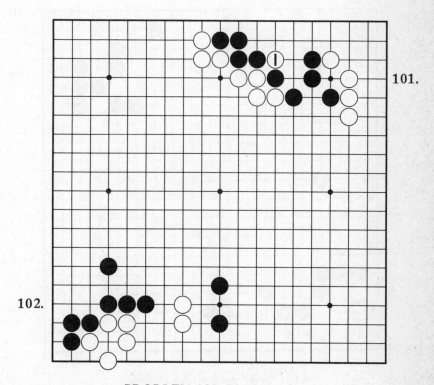

101.

102.

PROBLEM 102. Black to play.
Black can exploit a weakness in White's position and gain some profit.

PROBLEM 103. White to play.

The two black stones and three white stones on the outside are both vulnerable. How should White play?

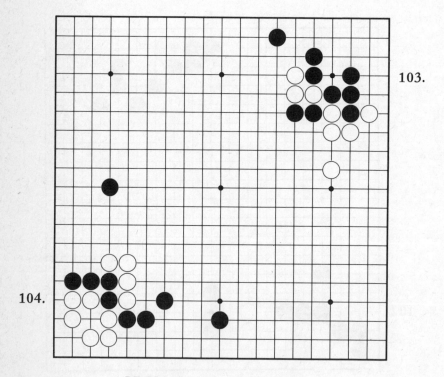

103.

104.

PROBLEM 104. Black to play.

How does Black link up his four stones on the lower left side to his stone above?

PROBLEM 105. *Black to play.*

There is a fight taking place at the top of the board. How does Black profit by sacrificing a stone? Indicate Black's next two moves.

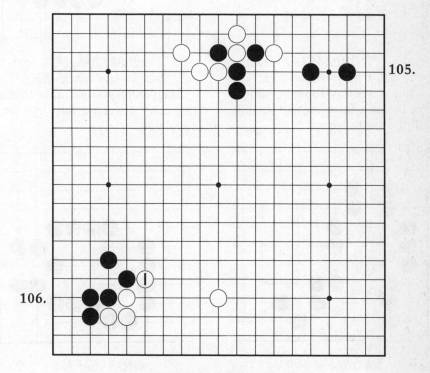

105.

106.

PROBLEM 106. *Black to play.*
How does Black respond to White 1?

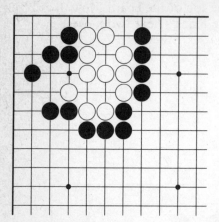

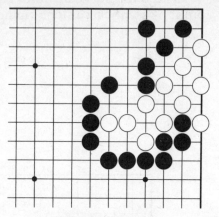

PROBLEM 107.
Black plays White dies.
There is a way to make White's eye below a false one and thereby kill the white group.

PROBLEM 108.
Black plays White dies.
Make sure you are able to distinguish between a false eye and a real eye.

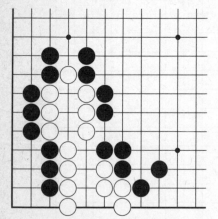

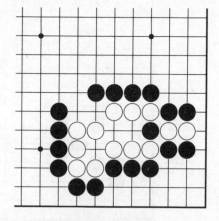

PROBLEM 109.
Black plays White dies.
Black's first move decides the fate of White's group.

PROBLEM 110
Black plays White dies.
By sacrificing a stone, Black can make one of White's eyes false and thereby kill the whole group.

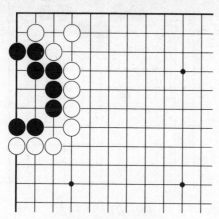

PROBLEM 111
White plays Black dies.
This is the basic 5-point nakade shape.

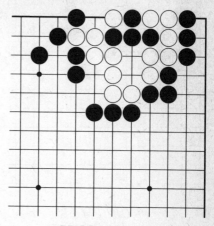

PROBLEM 112
Black plays White dies.
You can kill White by making a 5-point nakade shape.

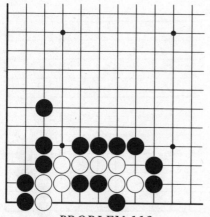

PROBLEM 113
Black plays White dies.
Black can kill White by sacrificing five stones.

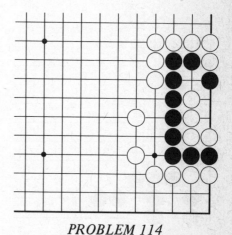

PROBLEM 114
Black plays and lives.
Black can live if he prevents White from making a 5-point nakade shape.

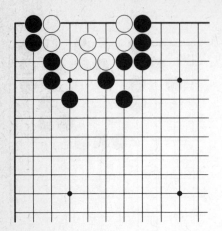

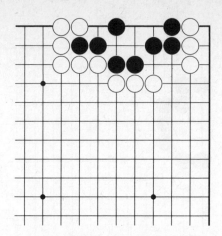

PROBLEM 115
Black plays White dies.

Because all the liberties on the outside of the two white stones on the left and the right are filled up, Black has a move to kill White.

PROBLEM 116
Black plays and lives.

Black must play on the correct point if he is to make two eyes and live.

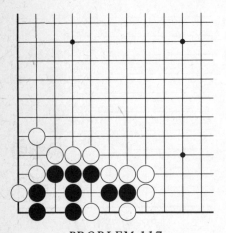

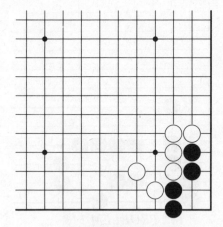

PROBLEM 117
Black plays and lives.

If Black can capture one white stone, he will live.

PROBLEM 118
Black plays and lives.

Where is the vital point that will give Black two eyes?

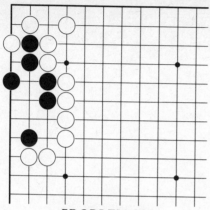

PROBLEM 119
Black plays and lives.

Without any doubt, Black has one eye. How can he make two eyes?

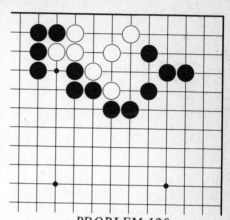

PROBLEM 120
Black plays White dies.

If you attack White's vital point, he will die.

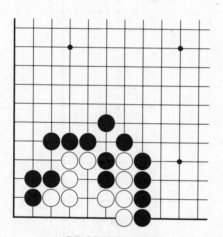

PROBLEM 121
White plays and lives.

White's first move will decide whether or not White can make two eyes.

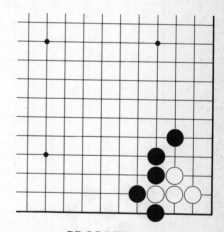

PROBLEM 122
Black plays White dies.

If you can prevent White from expanding his territory, he will not be able to make two eyes.

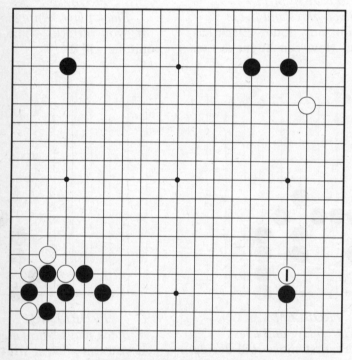

PROBLEM 123. Black to play.
White 1 is a ko threat. How should Black respond?

PROBLEM 124. *White to play.*

Black has cut with 1. How should White play so as to give his stones the best chance to make life?

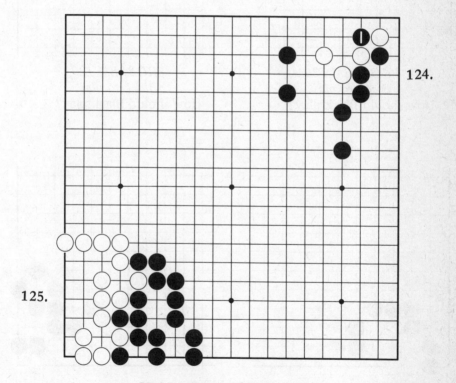

124.

125.

PROBLEM 125. *Black to play.*

Positions like this occur at the end of the game. Of the two kos, which one is the more profitable?

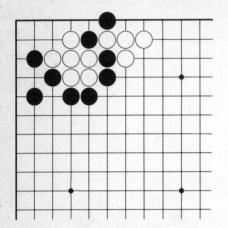

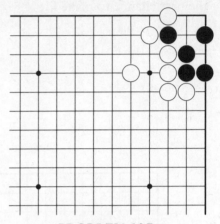

PROBLEM 126.
Black to play.
How should Black play?

PROBLEM 127.
Black to play.
How should Black play?

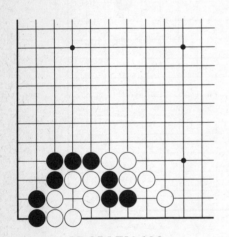

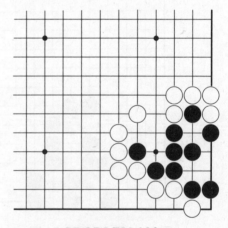

PROBLEM 128.
Black to play.
How can Black start a ko?

PROBLEM 129.
Black to play.
How should Black play?

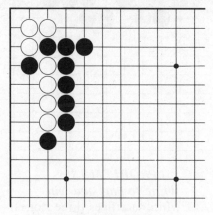

PROBLEM 130
Black to play and win.
Capture four white stones.

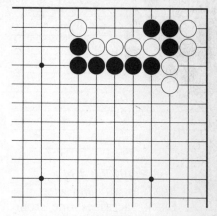

PROBLEM 131
Black to play and win.
Capture four white stones.

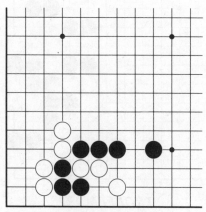

PROBLEM 132
Black to play and win.
Save the three black stones on the edge.

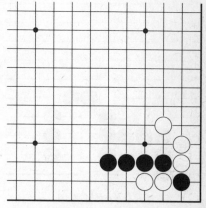

PROBLEM 133
Black to play and win.
Capture two white stones.

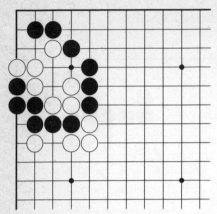

PROBLEM 134
Black to play and win.
If Black sacrifices one stone, he can capture seven white ones.

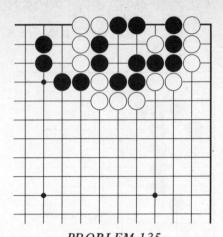

PROBLEM 135
White to play and win.
If White sacrifices three stones, he can capture all the black stones on the right.

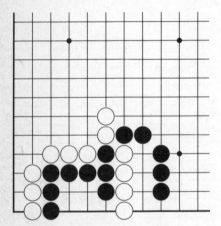

PROBLEM 136
Black to play and win.
Capture four white stones.

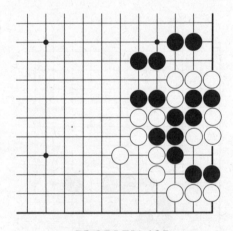

PROBLEM 137
Black to play and win.
A four-point nakade is worth five moves, so Black can win this capturing race.

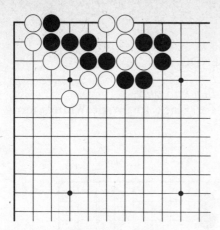

PROBLEM 138
Black to play and win.

"One eye beats no eyes." If you know this proverb, you shouldn't have any trouble capturing five white stones.

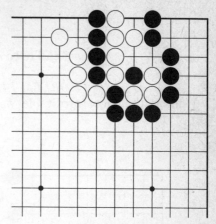

PROBLEM 139
Black to play and win.

Black can capture three white stones immediately, but this is not the problem. You want to capture all eight white stones.

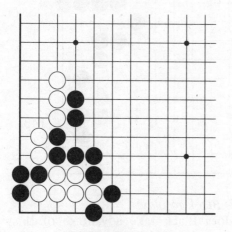

PROBLEM 140
Black to play and win.

If Black sacrifices one stone, he can capture six white ones.

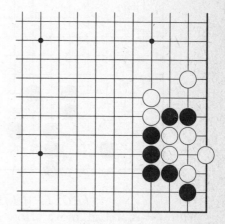

PROBLEM 141
Black to play and win.

The order of moves here is important if you want to capture the five white stones on the edge.

SECTION 7. ENDGAME

PROBLEM 142. Black to play.
What is the most profitable way for Black to invade White's territory?

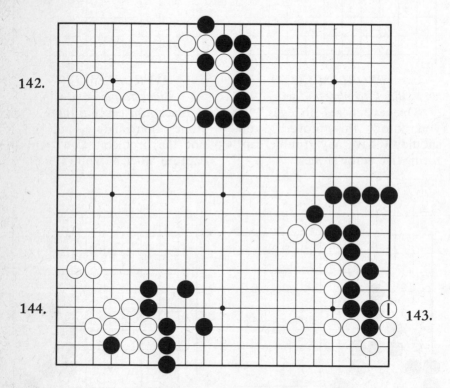

142.

144.

143.

PROBLEM 143. Black to play.
White 1 is a bad move. How does Black take advantage of this mistake?

PROBLEM 144. Black to play.
How does Black play to reduce White's territory on the left?

PROBLEMS 145 & 146. *White to play.*

How should White respond to the Black 1 in Problem 145 and the Black 1 in Problem 146? What is the difference between these two problems?

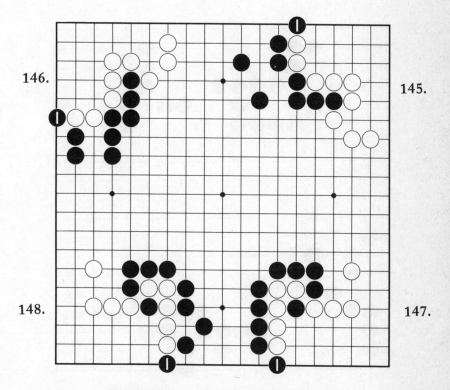

PROBLEMS 147 & 148. *White to play.*

How should White respond to the Black 1 in Problem 147 and the Black 1 in Problem 148? What is the difference between these two problems?

PROBLEM 149. Black to play.
Which is more profitable for Black, to play at A or to play at B?

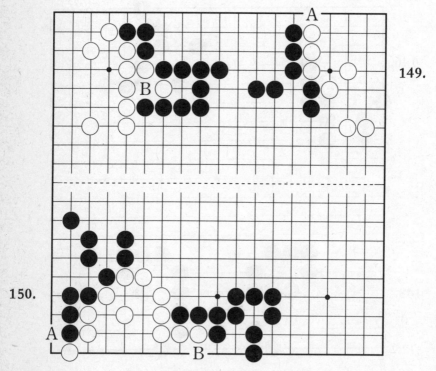

149.

150.

PROBLEM 150. Black to play.
Which is more profitable for Black, to play at A or to play at B?

III ELEMENTARY PROBLEMS
LEVEL THREE

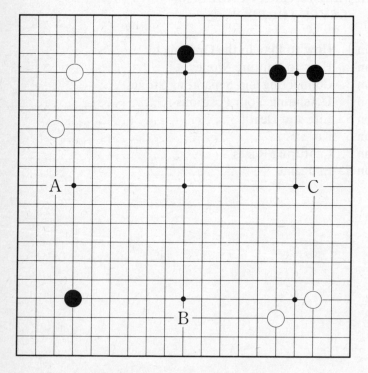

PROBLEM 151. Black to play.
Where should Black play, A, B or C?

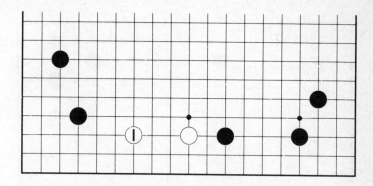

PROBLEM 152. Black to play.
When White plays 1, how should Black defend the corner?

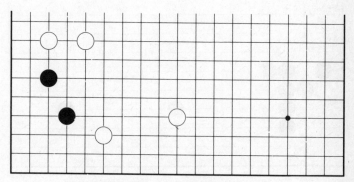

PROBLEM 153. Black to play.
How should Black defend his corner in this case?

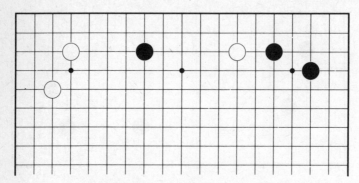

PROBLEM 154. White to play.
How should White play?

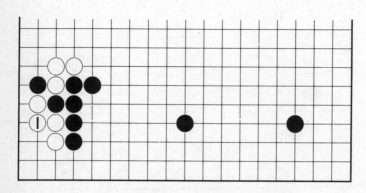

PROBLEM 155. Black to play.
How should Black play in response to White 1?

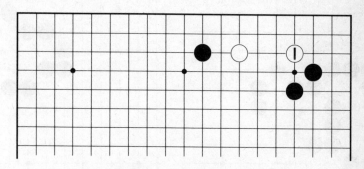

PROBLEM 156. Black to play.
How should Black respond to White 1?

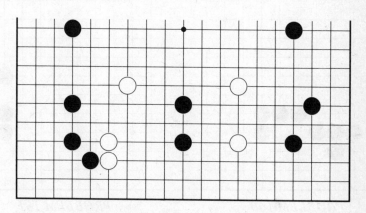

PROBLEM 157. Black to play.
In this 8-stone handicap game, how should Black play?

SECTION 2. HOW TO CAPTURE STONES

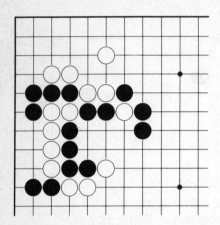

PROBLEM 158
Black to play.
How does Black save his four endangered stones in the center?

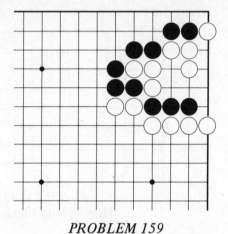

PROBLEM 159
Black to play.
How does Black play so as to capture three white stones?

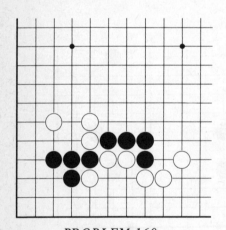

PROBLEM 160
Black to play.
How should Black play in this position?

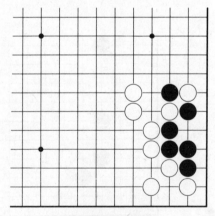

PROBLEM 161
White to play.
How should White play in this position?

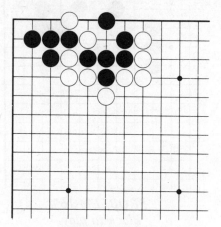

PROBLEM 162
White to play.
How should White play so as to capture five black stones?

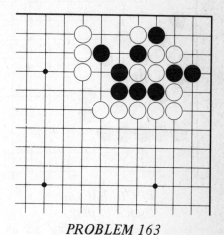

PROBLEM 163
Black to play.
How does Black play so as to capture four white stones?

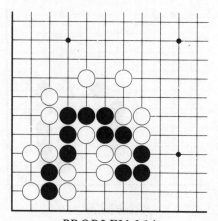

PROBLEM 164
Black to play.
How should Black play so as to capture four white stones?

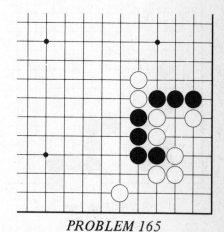

PROBLEM 165
Black to play.
How should Black play in this position?

SECTION 3. CONNECTING AND SEPARATING STONES

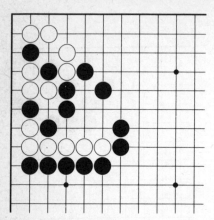

PROBLEM 166
Black to play.

How does Black play so as to prevent White from linking up his group at the bottom to the one at the top?

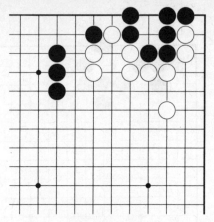

PROBLEM 167
Black to play.

How does Black play so as to link up his group at the top right to the stones on the left?

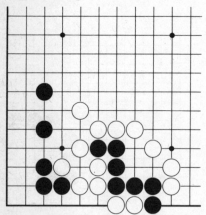

PROBLEM 168
Black to play.

How should Black play in this position?

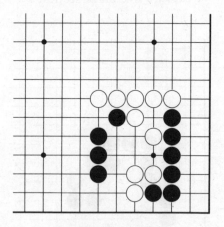

PROBLEM 169
Black to play.

How does Black play so as to cut off the white stones below from the ones above?

PROBLEM 170. Black to play.

Where should Black connect so as to isolate the seven white stones in the center?

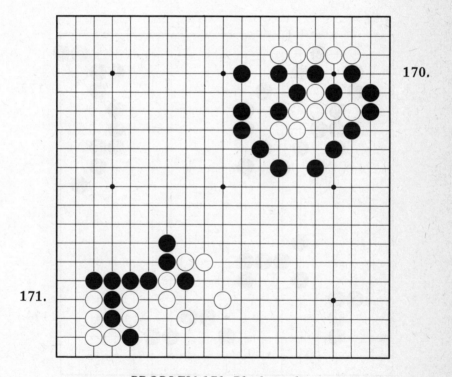

170.

171.

PROBLEM 171. Black to play.

Where should Black play so as to break into White's area at the bottom?

PROBLEM 172. Black to play.
How should Black play?

PROBLEM 173. Black to play.
How does Black play so as to save four of his surrounded stones?

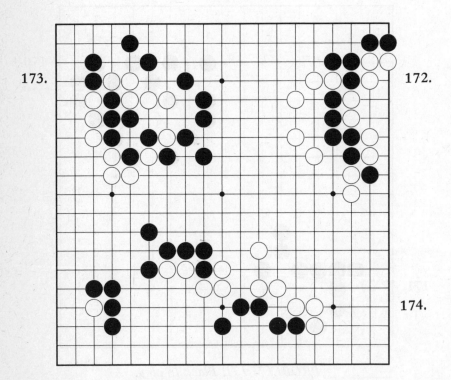

173.

172.

174.

PROBLEM 174. Black to play.
What is the most profitable way for Black to play?

SECTION 4. DEFENDING YOUR POSITIONS

PROBLEM 175. Black to play.
How should Black respond to White 1?

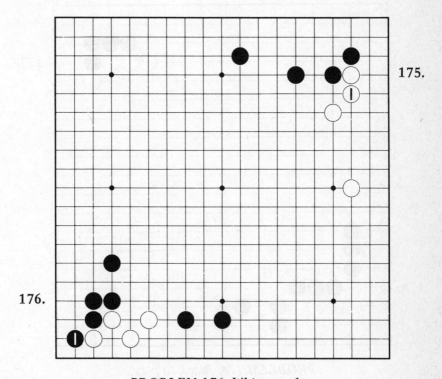

175.

176.

PROBLEM 176. White to play.
How should White respond to Black 1?

PROBLEM 177. Black to play.

Defending the corner on the right is not important. How should Black play?

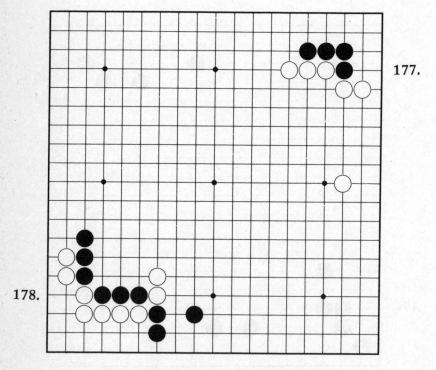

177.

178.

PROBLEM 178. Black to play.

Black has to give his six stones on the outside good shape. Where should he play?

PROBLEM 179. White to play.

Where is the vital point to attack the four black stones on the left?

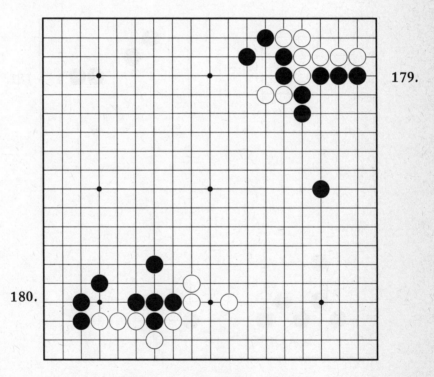

179.

180.

PROBLEM 180. Black to play.

White has a defect in his position. Where is the vital point for breaking into White's area? You can capture at least one white stone.

PROBLEM 181. Black to play.
How should Black respond to White 1?

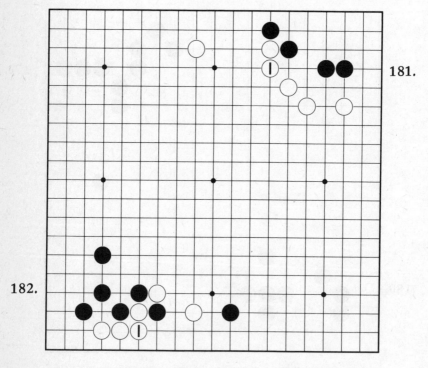

181.

182.

PROBLEM 182. Black to play.
How should Black respond to White 1?

PROBLEM 183. Black to play.
How should Black respond to White's peep at 1?

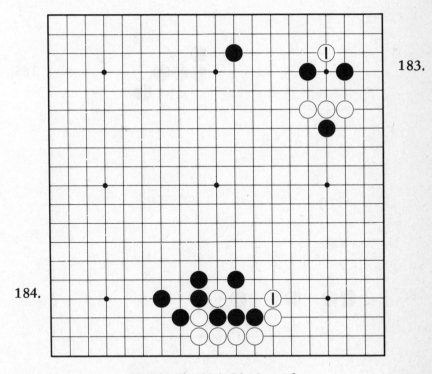

183.

184.

PROBLEM 184. Black to play.
How should Black respond to White 1?

PROBLEM 185. White to play.
How should White respond to Black 1?

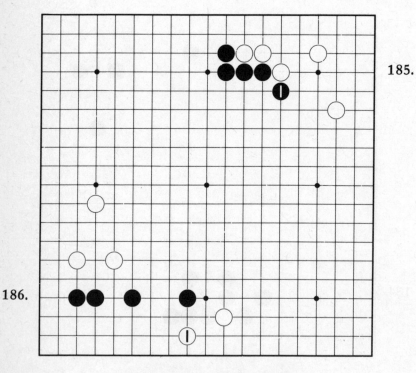

185.

186.

PROBLEM 186. Black to play.
How should Black respond to White 1?

PROBLEM 187. White to play.
How should White play?

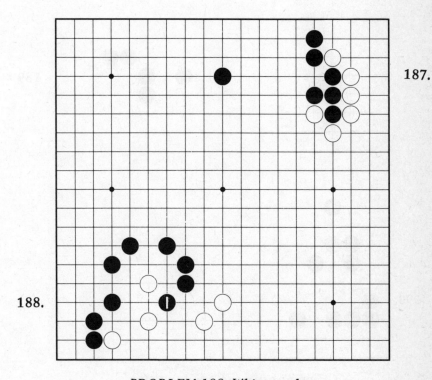

187.

188.

PROBLEM 188. White to play.
How should White respond to Black 1?

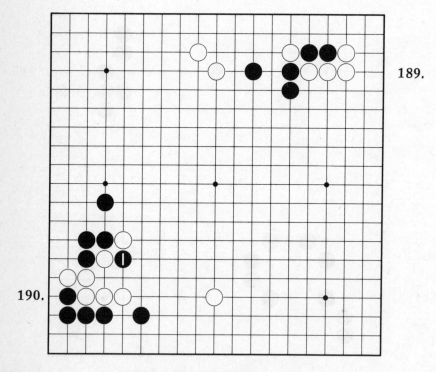

189.

190.

PROBLEM 190. *White to play.*
How should White respond to Black 1?

PROBLEM 191. Black to play.
How should Black play so as to separate White into two groups?

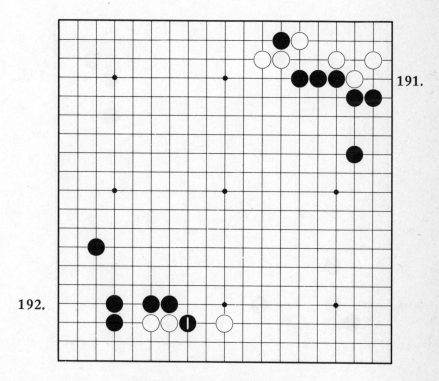

191.

192.

PROBLEM 192. White to play.
How should White respond to Black 1?

PROBLEM 193. Black to play.
Where is the invasion point in White's position?

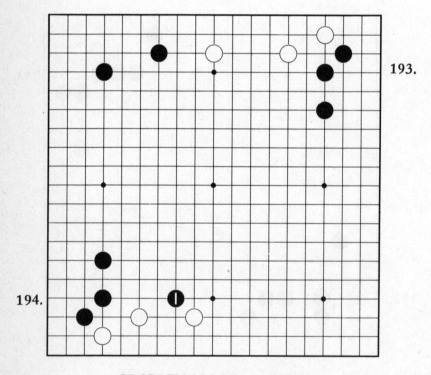

193.

194.

PROBLEM 194. White to play.
How should White respond to Black 1?

PROBLEM 195. White to play.
White can give atari immediately and sacrifice one stone. But is this the most effective way to sacrifice? How should White play?

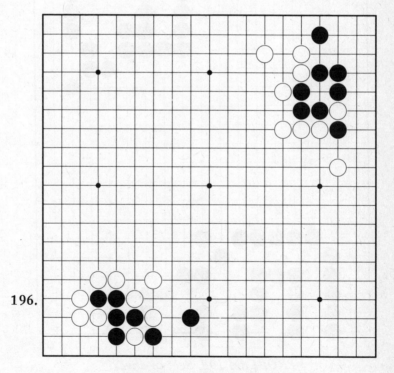

195.

196.

PROBLEM 196. White to play.
How should White play?

SECTION 5. LIFE AND DEATH

PROBLEM 197. Can stones be captured?
The situation at the top is a seki, but Black can still capture some
white stones. How many stones can Black capture?

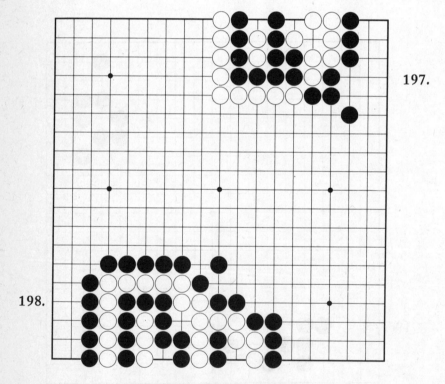

197.

198.

PROBLEM 198. Seki or alive?
Is this position a seki? If not a seki, which side can capture the other
side's stones?

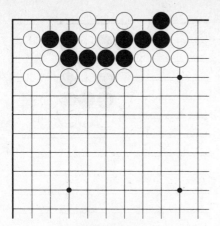

PROBLEM 199
Black plays and lives.
How does Black play so as to live?

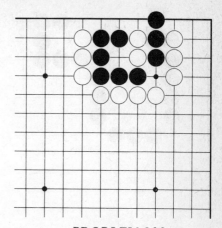

PROBLEM 200
Black plays and lives.
How does Black play so as to live?

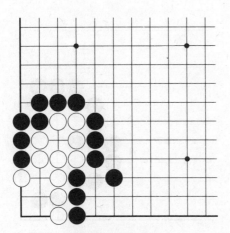

PROBLEM 201
Black plays and gets a seki.
How does Black play so as to get a seki?

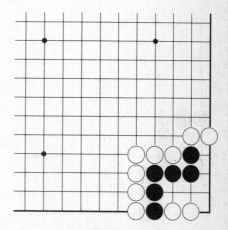

PROBLEM 202
Black plays and lives.
How does Black play so as to live?

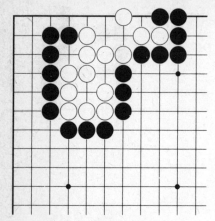

PROBLEM 203
Black plays White dies.
Kill the white group by making the eye at the top false.

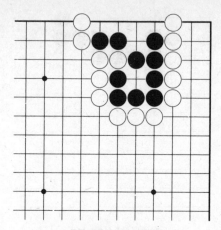

PROBLEM 204
Black plays and lives.
Give the black group life by making an eye at the top.

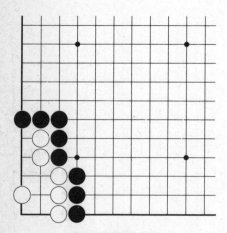

PROBLEM 205
Black plays White dies.
By sacrificing a stone, Black can kill the white group.

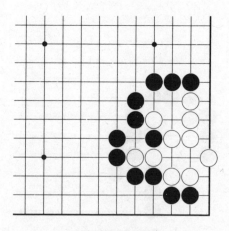

PROBLEM 206
Black plays White dies.
By sacrificing a stone, Black can kill the white group.

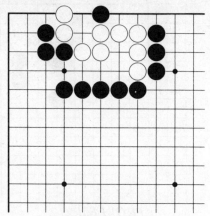

PROBLEM 207
Black plays White dies.
A brilliant first move kills the white group.

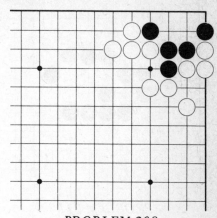

PROBLEM 208
Black plays and lives.
A brilliant first move give the black group life.

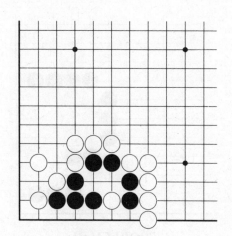

PROBLEM 209
Black plays and lives.
Black's first move is all-important.

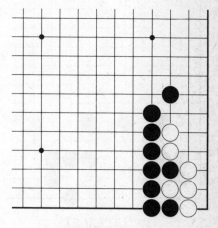

PROBLEM 210
Black plays White dies.
Black's first move is all-important.

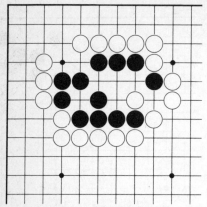

PROBLEM 211
White plays Black dies.
White's first move is all-important.

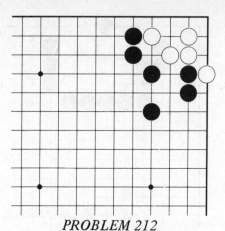

PROBLEM 212
Black plays White dies.
If you attack the vital points of White's group in the proper order, White will die.

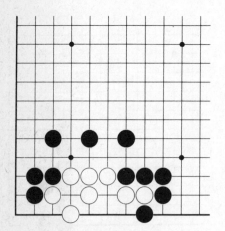

PROBLEM 213
Black plays White dies.
You have to be careful not to let White live by sacrificing two stones.

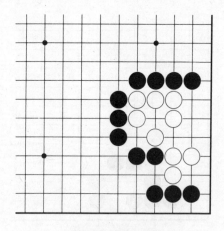

PROBLEM 214
Black plays White dies.
By attacking the right point with the first move, the fate of the white group is decided.

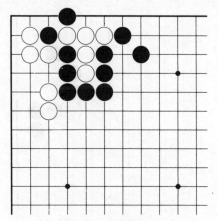

PROBLEM 215
Black plays and makes a ko.
How can Black make a ko?

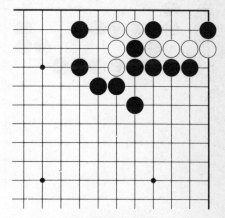

PROBLEM 216
Black plays and makes a ko.
How can Black make a ko?

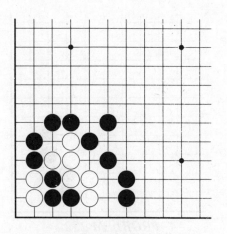

PROBLEM 217
Black plays and makes a ko.
Decide the life or death of the
white group with a ko.

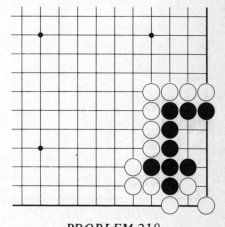

PROBLEM 218
Black plays and makes a ko.
Black's only chance to live is
to make a ko.

SECTION 7. CAPTURING RACES

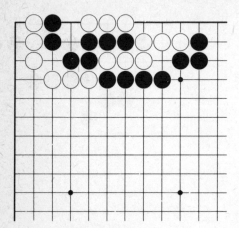

PROBLEM 219
Black to play.

How can Black capture the nine white stones on the right?

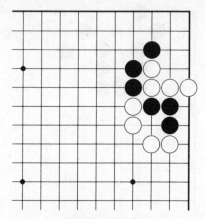

PROBLEM 220
Black to play.

How can Black capture the four white stones at the top?

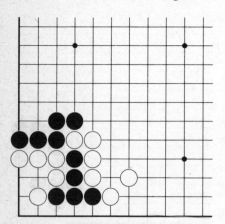

PROBLEM 221
Black to play.

A brilliant first move will capture the white stones in the corner.

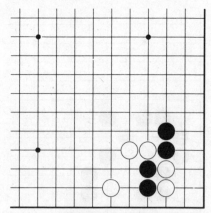

PROBLEM 222
Black to play.

A brilliant first move will capture the two white stones in the corner.

"One eye beats no eye." If you understand this proverb, you will immediately see how to capture the four white stones on the right.

PROBLEM 224. *Black to play.*
Capture five white stones in the top left corner.

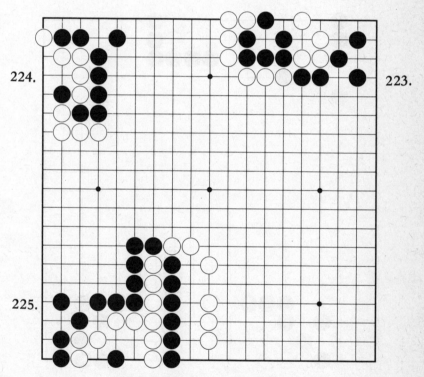

PROBLEM 225. *White to play.*
"A five-point nakade is worth eight liberties." This knowledge will help you find a way to capture the six black stones on the right.

SECTION 8. ENDGAME

PROBLEM 226. Black to play.
There is a defect in White's position. Playing at the right point will allow you to reduce White's territory by capturing some stones.

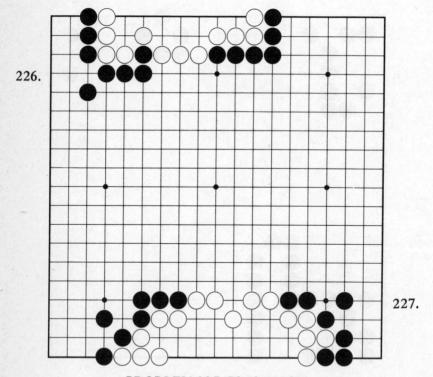

226.

227.

PROBLEM 227. Black to play.
There is a defect in White's position. Playing at the right point will allow you to reduce White's territory by capturing some stones.

PROBLEM 228. Black to play.

What are Black's most profitable endgame moves to reduce White's territory?

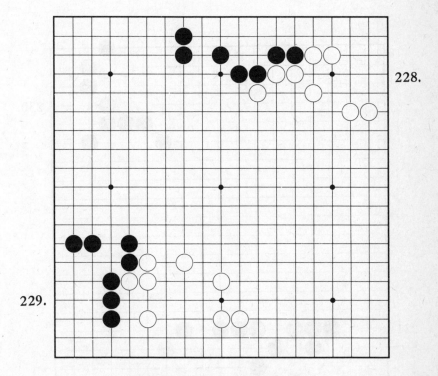

228.

229.

PROBLEM 229. White to play.

What are White's most profitable endgame moves to reduce Black's territory?

PROBLEM 230. Black to play.

If you play correctly, you can make a big dent in White's territory because the three white stones on the far right will be short of liberties. Where is the vital point?

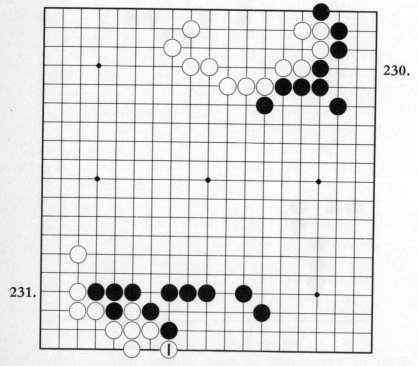

230.

231.

PROBLEM 231. Black to play.
How should Black respond to White 1?

IV ELEMENTARY PROBLEMS
LEVEL FOUR
LIFE AND DEATH PROBLEMS

SECTION 1. MAKING LIFE

PROBLEM 232. Black to play and live. (1 move)
First of all Black has to make one eye. After that his second eye cannot be blocked.

PROBLEM 233. Black to play and live. (1 move)
Two eyes can be made with one move.

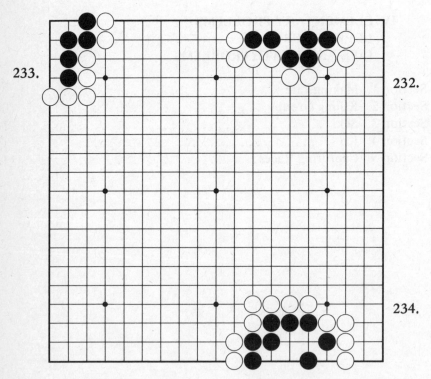

233.

232.

234.

PROBLEM 234. Black to play and live. (1 move)
Two eyes can be made with one move.

PROBLEM 235. Black to play and live. (1 move)
If Black takes the one white stone in the right way, he can secure life for his group.

PROBLEM 236. Black to play and live. (1 move)
If Black attacks the lone white stone in the right way, he can secure life for his group.

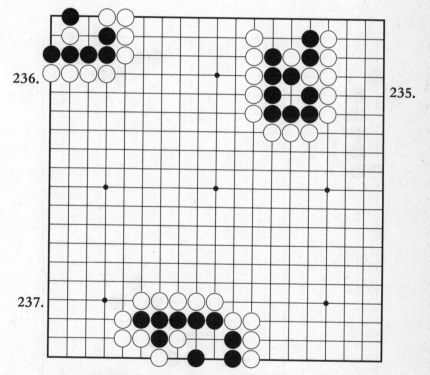

PROBLEM 237. Black to play and live. (1 move)
If Black gives atari to White in the right way, he can secure life for his group.

PROBLEM 238. Black to play and live. (1 move)
Black can secure life with his first move.

PROBLEM 239. Black to play and live. (1 move)
Black can secure life with his first move.

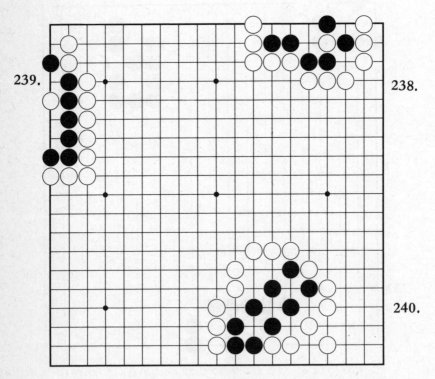

239.

238.

240.

PROBLEM 240. Black to play and live. (1 move)
Where does Black play to make two eyes?

PROBLEM 241. White to play and live. (1 move)
White can make life in two ways. Which way is the more profitable?

PROBLEM 242. White to play and live. (1 move)
If you can make a real eye on the right, the white group can live.

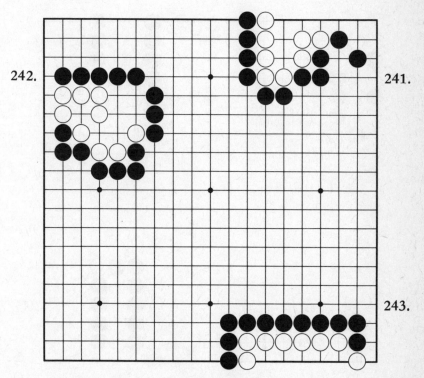

242.

241.

243.

PROBLEM 243. White to play and live. (1 move)
White can make life in two ways. Which way is the more profitable?

PROBLEM 244. Black to play and live. (1 move)
If Black gives atari to the three white stones in the right way, his group will live.

PROBLEM 245. Black to play and live. (1 move)
If Black gives atari to the white stone in the right way, his group will live.

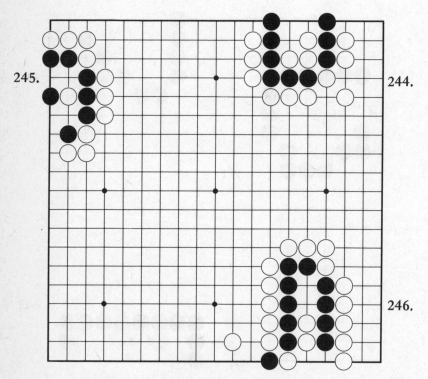

PROBLEM 246. Black to play and live. (1 move)
If Black simply captures a stone, he will die.

PROBLEM 247. Black to play and live. (1 move)
You don't have to think very hard to find a move that will make two
eyes for Black's group.

PROBLEM 248. Black to play and live. (3 moves)
With the right move, Black can live.

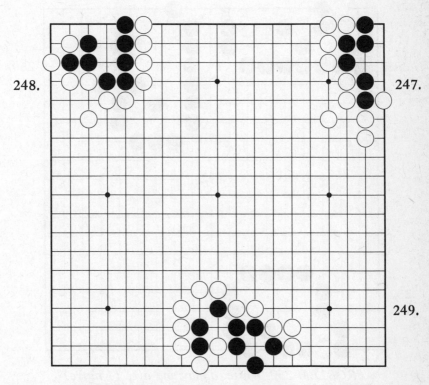

248.

247.

249.

PROBLEM 249. Black to play and live. (3 moves)
If Black can capture a white stone, he will live.

PROBLEM 250. White to play and live. (1 move)
Three of White's stones are in atari. If White takes a black stone, can he live?

PROBLEM 251. White to play and live. (1 move)
White can live if he captures the two black stones on the edge in the right way.

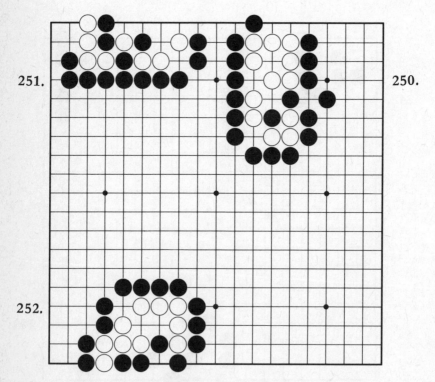

251.   250.

252.

PROBLEM 252. White to play and live. (1 move)
By using the oiotoshi technique, you can secure life for the white stones.

PROBLEM 253. Black to play and live. (3 moves)
Can Black take the one white stone that is in atari?

PROBLEM 254. Black to play and live. (1 move)
Can Black live by capturing two stones?

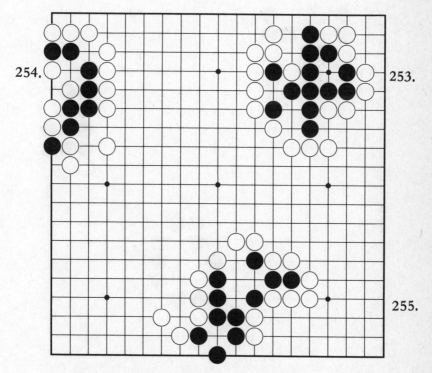

PROBLEM 255. Black to play and live. (1 move)
If Black is going to live, he has to sacrifice two stones.

PROBLEM 256. Black to play and live. (1 move)
If Black immediately takes the four white stones, will he live?

PROBLEM 257. Black to play and live. (1 move)
If you play on the vital point of the five-point nakade, Black will live.

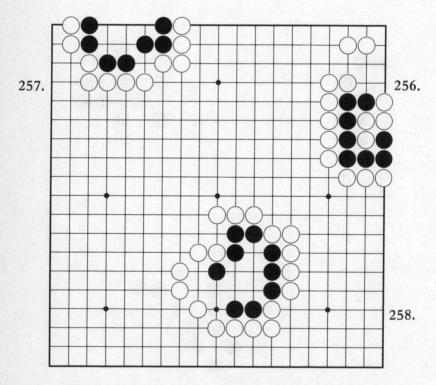

PROBLEM 258. Black to play and live. (1 move)
The first thing Black has to do in order to live is to make one real eye.

PROBLEM 259. Black to play and live. (1 move)
Black has to secure another eye at the top in order to live.

PROBLEM 260. Black to play and live. (1 move)
You can secure life for the black stones on the first move.

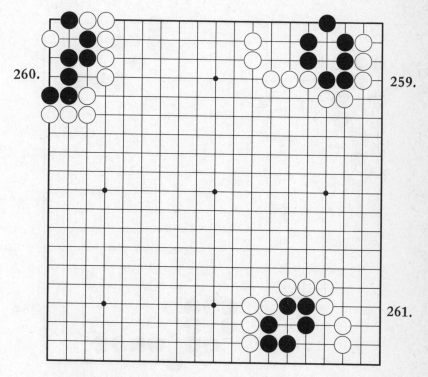

260.

259.

261.

PROBLEM 261. Black to play and live. (1 move)
If you can make another eye, Black's group will live.

PROBLEM 262. Black to play and live. (1 move)
The first move secures life for the black group.

PROBLEM 263. Black to play and live. (1 move)
If you give atari to the white stone, the black group will die.

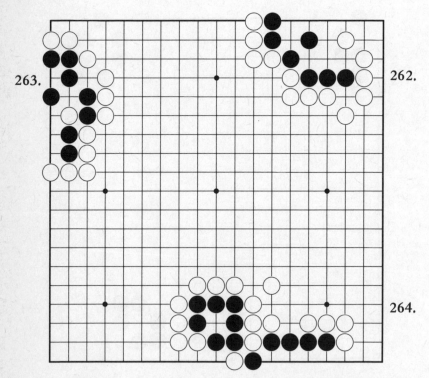

263.

262.

264.

PROBLEM 264. Black to play and live. (1 move)
If you capture the white stone on the edge, the black group will die.

PROBLEM 265. Black to play and live. (3 moves)
If you play the first move correctly, Black will have no trouble living.

PROBLEM 266. Black to play and live. (1 move)
The first move decides whether or not the black group lives.

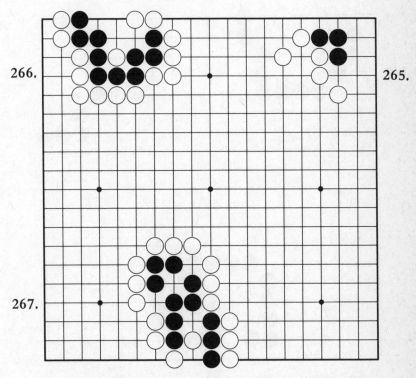

PROBLEM 267. Black to play and live. (1 move)
If you can capture one white stone, Black's group will live.

SECTION 2. KILLING GROUPS

PROBLEM 268. Black plays White dies. (1 move)
If you play on the vital point of the 5-point nakade, White will die.

PROBLEM 269. Black plays White dies. (1 move)
Where is the vital point to prevent White from making two eyes?

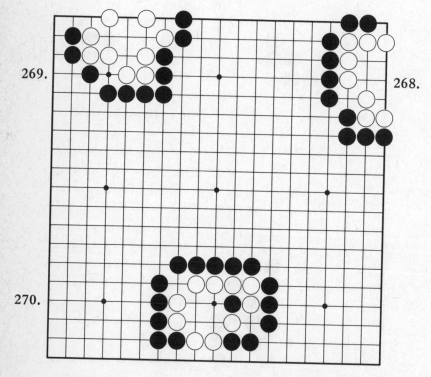

PROBLEM 270. Black plays White dies. (1 move)
Black is going to have to sacrifice three stones in order to kill White.

PROBLEM 271. Black plays White dies. (1 move)
Even though White can capture a stone, that point will become a false eye.

PROBLEM 272. Black plays White dies. (3 moves)
Kill all the white stones!

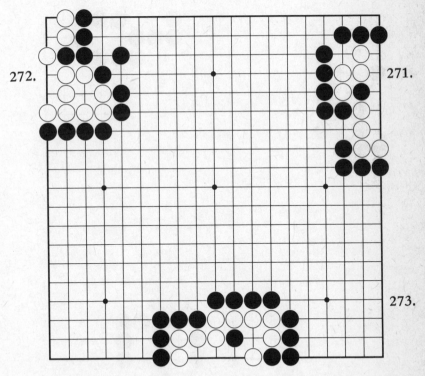

272.

271.

273.

PROBLEM 273. Black plays White dies. (1 move)
You can kill White by forcing him to make a three-point nakade.

PROBLEM 274. White plays Black dies. (3 moves)
Because of the lone white stone inside Black's area, White has a move
to kill the black group.

PROBLEM 275. White plays Black dies. (3 moves)
White can kill Black by sacrificing two stones.

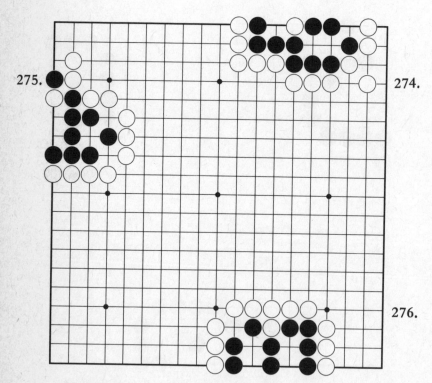

275.   274.

                                                                   276.

PROBLEM 276. White plays Black dies. (3 moves)
White can kill Black by sacrificing a stone.

PROBLEM 277. Black plays White dies. (3 moves)
If you sacrifice the black stone in atari in the right way, you can kill the white group.

PROBLEM 278. Black plays White dies. (3 moves)
If you sacrifice the black stone in atari in the right way, you can kill the white group.

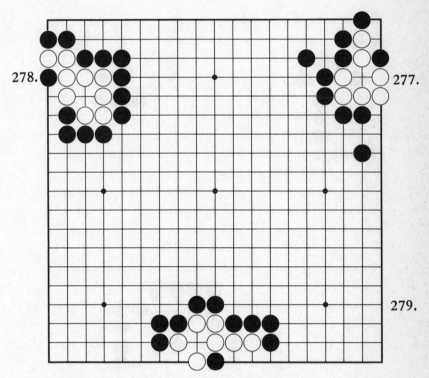

PROBLEM 279. Black plays White dies. (1 move)
A quiet move kills the white group.

PROBLEM 280. Black plays White dies. (1 move)
If you play on the point where White would play, the white group dies.

PROBLEM 281. Black plays White dies. (3 moves)
You have to sacrifice three stones in order to kill White.

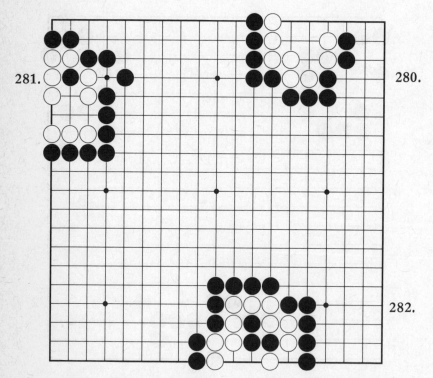

281.

280.

282.

PROBLEM 282. Black plays White dies. (3 moves)
Make a four-point nakade and you will kill White.

PROBLEM 283. Black plays White dies. (3 moves)
There are two moves which can be played in any order that kill White.

PROBLEM 284. Black plays White dies. (1 move)
Putting two stones in atari is not enough to kill White.

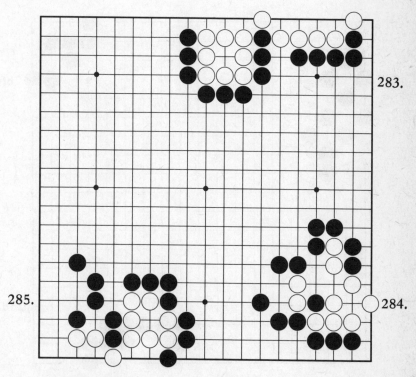

283.

285.

284.

PROBLEM 285. Black plays White dies. (3 moves)
Black must first defend his weak point. After that it is easy to kill White.

PROBLEM 286. White plays Black dies. (3 moves)
If you make a 'bent four in the corner', Black dies.

PROBLEM 287. White plays Black dies. (1 move)
Where is the point that makes all but one of Black's potential eyes false?

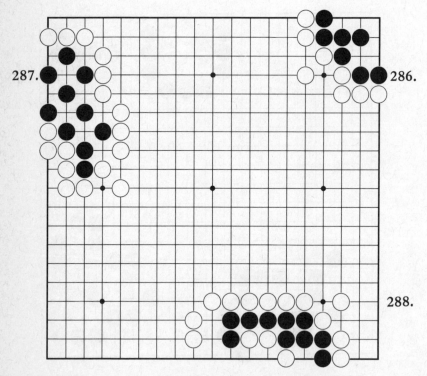

PROBLEM 288. White plays Black dies. (3 moves)
If you make a five-point nakade, Black will die. A ko is not good enough.

PROBLEM 289. Black plays White dies. (1 move)
In order to kill White you have to prevent him from making an eye in the corner.

PROBLEM 290. Black plays White dies. (3 moves)
If you play on the vital point, it will be easy to kill White.

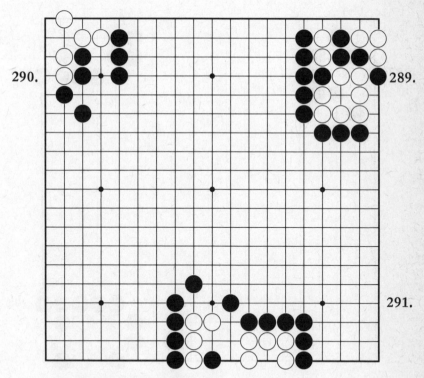

290.

289.

291.

PROBLEM 291. Black plays White dies. (3 moves)
Make a shape in which White is unable to move.

PROBLEM 292. Black plays White dies. (3 moves)
Because White is short of liberties, there is a way to kill his stones.

PROBLEM 293. Black plays White dies. (3 moves)
In order to kill White, does Black defend or attack?

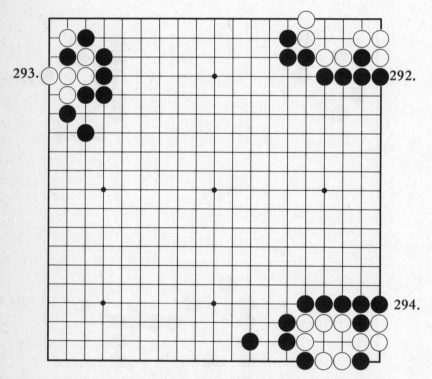

PROBLEM 294. Black plays White dies. (1 move)
Because White is short of liberties, there is a way to kill his stones.

PROBLEM 295. Black plays White dies. (3 moves)
First of all, Black has to destroy White's eye shape.

PROBLEM 296. Black plays White dies. (3 moves)
If you reduce the size of White's area, you can easily kill his stones.

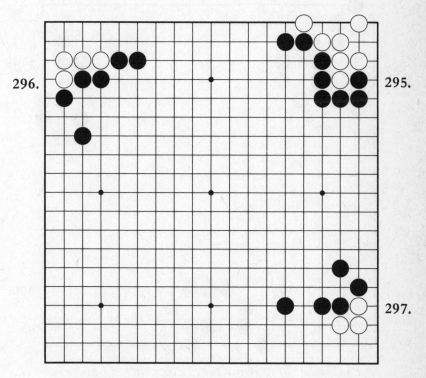

296.

295.

297.

PROBLEM 297. Black plays White dies. (1 move)
If you reduce the size of White's area, you can easily kill his stones.

PROBLEM 298. White plays Black dies. (3 moves)
By exploiting the shortage of liberties of the three black stones at the top, you can kill Black.

PROBLEM 299. White plays Black dies. (1 move)
Black will die if you can prevent him from making an eye at the top.

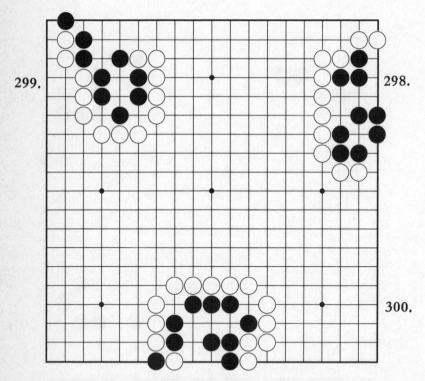

PROBLEM 300. White plays Black dies. (1 move)
It is not necessary to capture the black stone in order to kill Black's group.

PROBLEM 301. Black plays White dies. (1 move)
By sacrificing one stone, Black can kill White.

PROBLEM 302. Black plays White dies. (3 moves)
By sacrificing one stone, Black can kill White.

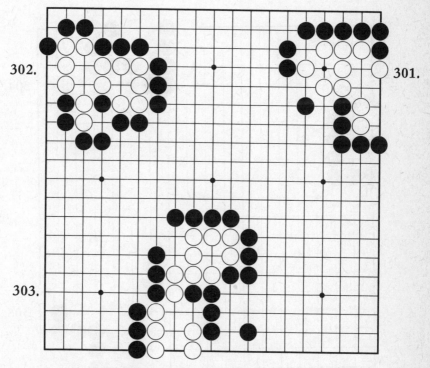

PROBLEM 303. Black plays White dies. (5 moves)
In order to kill White, Black first of all has to sacrifice two stones
followed by a one-stone sacrifice.

SECTION 3. SEKI

PROBLEM 304. Black plays and gets a seki. (1 move)
It is impossible for White to kill Black by sacrificing four stones.

PROBLEM 305. Black plays and gets a seki. (3 moves)
It is impossible for White to kill Black by sacrificing four stones.

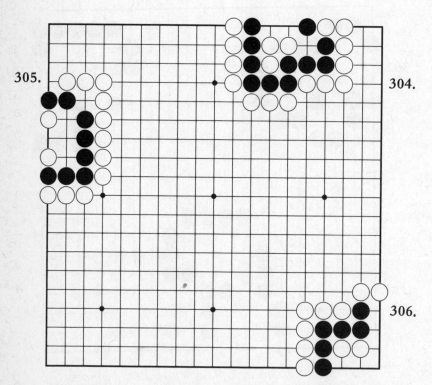

PROBLEM 306. Black plays and gets a seki. (3 moves)
In this position a false eye is good enough for a seki.

PROBLEM 307. White plays and gets a seki. (1 move)
If you don't try to capture the two black stones, you can get a seki.

PROBLEM 308. White plays and gets a seki. (1 move)
Make a seki between the five black stones and the three white ones.

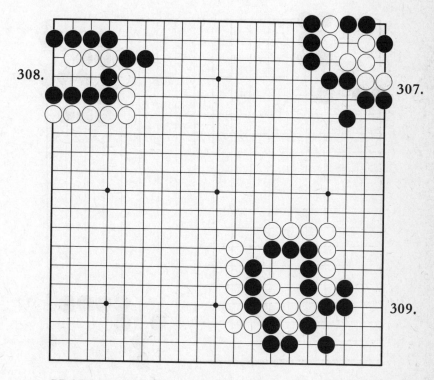

308.

307.

309.

PROBLEM 309. White plays and gets a seki. (3 moves)
Make a seki between the central white and black stones.

SECTION 4. KO

PROBLEM 310. Black plays and makes a ko. (2 moves)
Make a ko in the corner.

PROBLEM 311. Black plays and makes a ko. (3 moves)
Make a ko for the life or death of the white group in the corner.

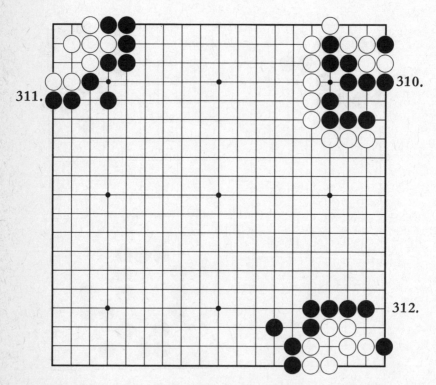

311.

310.

312.

PROBLEM 312. Black plays and makes a ko. (4 moves)
Make a ko for the life or death of the white group in the corner.

PROBLEM 313. Black plays and makes a ko. (3 moves)
Make a ko for the life or death of the white group.

PROBLEM 314. Black plays and makes a ko. (4 moves)
If Black sacrifices a stone, he can get a ko.

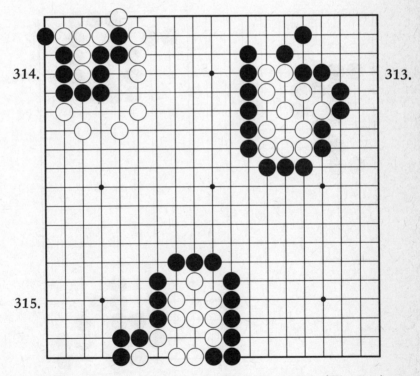

314.

313.

315.

PROBLEM 315. Black plays and makes a ko. (3 moves)
If Black sacrifices a stone, he can get a ko for the life or death of the white group.

SECTION 5. CAPTURING RACES

PROBLEM 316. Black to play and win. (1 move)
How does Black capture seven white stones?

PROBLEM 317. Black to play and win. (1 move)
How does Black capture five white stones?

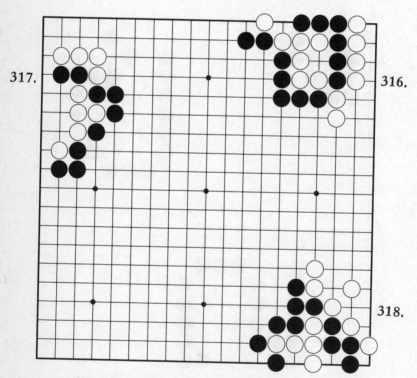

PROBLEM 318. Black to play and win. (1 move)
How does Black capture five white stones?

PROBLEM 319. White to play and win. (1 move)
'One eye beats no eyes'. Capture the six black stones!

PROBLEM 320. White to play and win. (1 move)
Make an eye and capture six black stones.

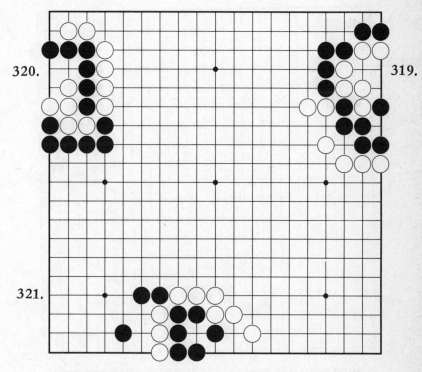

320.   319.

321.

PROBLEM 321. White to play and win. (1 move)
How does White capture six black stones?

PROBLEM 322. Black to play and win. (3 moves)
Can Black save his five endangered stones?

PROBLEM 323. Black to play and win. (3 moves)
How does Black play so as to capture the four white stones in the corner?

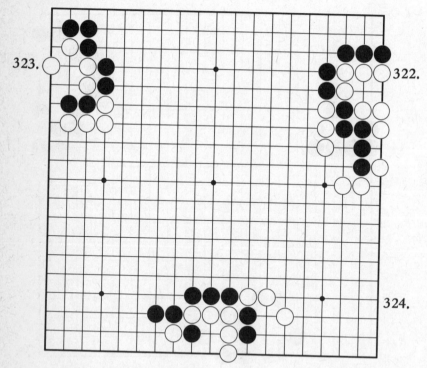

PROBLEM 324. Black to play and win. (1 move)
If Black makes a brilliant move, six white stones will die.

PROBLEM 325. White to play and win. (1 move)
How does White play so as to capture five black stones?

PROBLEM 326. White to play and win. (3 moves)
If White sacrifices a stone, he can capture six black stones.

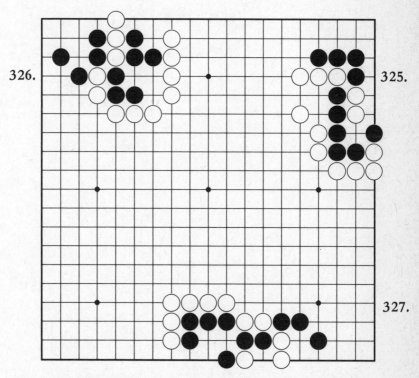

326.

325.

327.

PROBLEM 327. White to play and win. (3 moves)
If White sacrifices a stone, he can capture seven black stones.

PART TWO

ANSWERS

PROBLEM 1

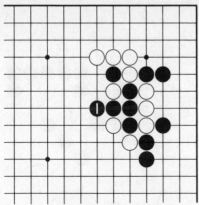

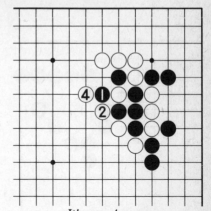

Correct Answer
By playing at 1, Black rescues his four endangered stones. Now the three white stones on the right are doomed.

Wrong Answer
3 connects to the right of 1
Capturing a stone with 1 fails. After giving atari with 2 and 4, White will capture seven black stones.

PROBLEM 2

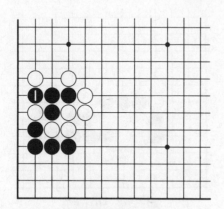

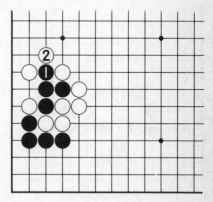

Correct Answer
By giving atari to a white stone with 1, Black can save his three endangered stones.

Wrong Answer
If Black plays 1, White blocks the escape route with 2 and the four black stones will be captured on the next move.

PROBLEM 3

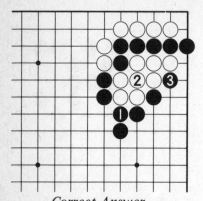

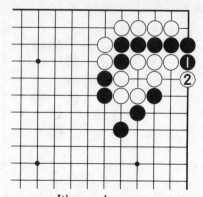

Correct Answer

Giving atari with Black 1 is the correct answer. If White connects at 2, he can't escape after 3.

Wrong Answer

If Black plays 1, White 2 puts seven black stones into atari. Black has failed.

PROBLEM 4

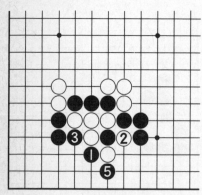

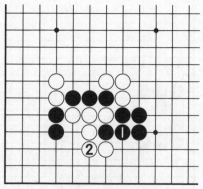

Correct Answer
4 connects to the left of 2

First of all, Black gives atari with 1 and 3. Now, with the atari of 5, it becomes a ladder and White cannot escape.

Wrong Answer

Connecting with Black 1 lets White off the hook. After White connects at 2, he cannot be captured.

PROBLEM 5

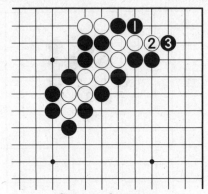

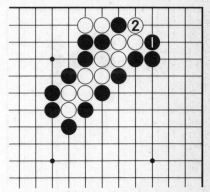

Correct Answer
If Black plays 1 and 3, the ten white stones can't avoid capture.

Wrong Answer
Playing at 1 here allows White to catch a black stone with 2 and thereby escape.

PROBLEM 6

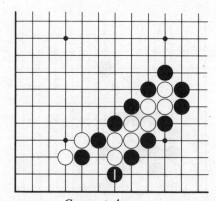

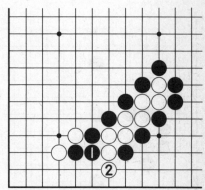

Correct Answer
If Black plays 1, the eight white stones can be captured on the next move.

Wrong Answer
Giving atari with 1 here fails. White extends to 2, leaving Black with too many defects in his position to defend properly.

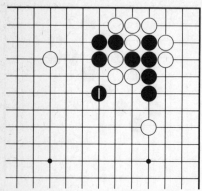

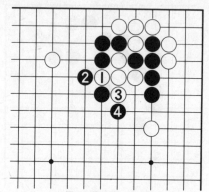

Correct Answer

If Black plays 1, the three white stones in the center cannot escape.

For Reference

If White tries to escape with 1 and 3, Black blocks with 2 and 4, so there is no way to avoid capture.

PROBLEM 8

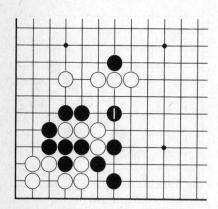

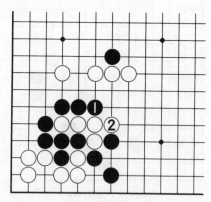

Correct Answer

If Black plays 1, the four white stones cannot escape.

Wrong Answer

Giving atari with 1 here fails. White extends to 2 and can no longer be captured.

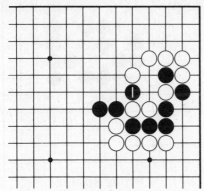

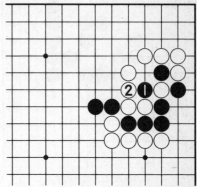

Correct Answer	Wrong Answer
Black 1 captures two white stones, so the four black stones on the right will link up to the two in the center.	Black 1 may capture a stone, but after White plays 2 the seven black stones on the right are dead.

PROBLEM 10

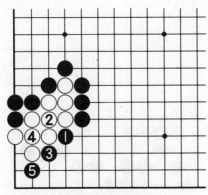

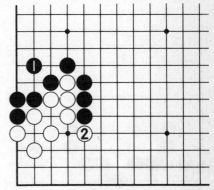

Correct Answer	Wrong Answer
Giving atari with 1 is the correct answer. White's attempt to save his stones with 2 and 4 is futile: after Black 5, ten white stones will be captured.	Defending with 1 is wrong. White defends his position with 2. The white stones are now safe.

PROBLEM 11

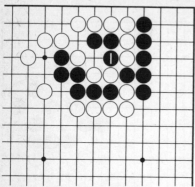

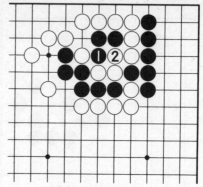

Correct Answer

Black can save his eight endangered stones by giving atari to two white stones with 1. These two stones cannot avoid being captured.

Wrong Answer

Giving atari with Black 1 here fails. After White connects with 2, the nine black stones are dead.

PROBLEM 12

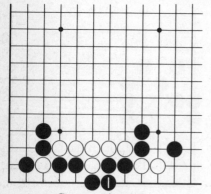

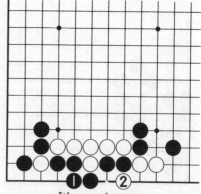

Correct Answer

Black 1 is the right move. The black stones on the edge can no longer be captured.

Wrong Answer

Connecting with Black 1 here fails. Because of a shortage of liberties, Black cannot defend his two stones in atari.

PROBLEM 13

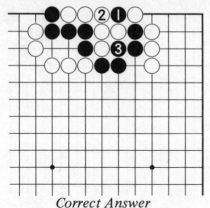 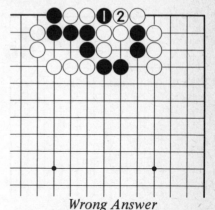

Correct Answer

Black 1 and 3 are the moves that capture six white stones.

Wrong Answer

If Black immediately captures two white stones with 1, White will connect at 2. The six black stones at the top are now dead.

PROBLEM 14

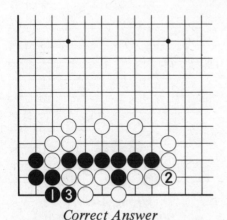 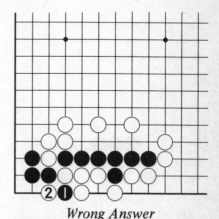

Correct Answer

After 1 and 3, there is no way for the four white stones that are in atari to escape capture.

Wrong Answer

Black 1 fails. After White takes with 2, the best Black can hope for is a ko.

PROBLEM 15

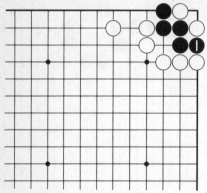

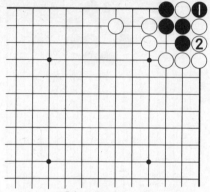

Correct Answer

Black 1 captures the two white stones in the corner. Note that White cannot connect at the 1−1 point (oshitsubushi), so Black lives with two eyes.

Wrong Answer

Capturing one stone with Black 1 fails. Black dies after White plays 2.

PROBLEM 16

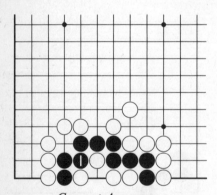

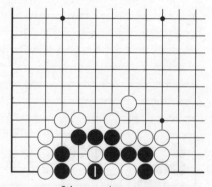

Correct Answer

Black 1 again creates an oshitsubushi shape, so the four white stones in atari will be captured.

Wrong Answer
2 retakes to the right of 1

If Black takes two stones with 1, White retakes with 2. Black is dead because he will eventually be reduced to one eye.

PROBLEM 17

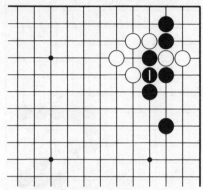

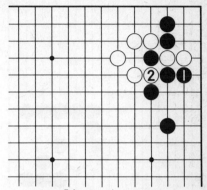

Correct Answer
If Black connects at 1, he will eventually be able to capture the two white stones on the right.

Wrong Answer
If Black plays at 1, White cuts off one black stone with 2, so now the two white stones cannot be captured.

PROBLEM 18

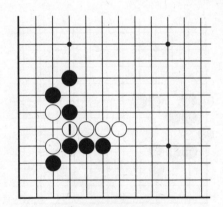

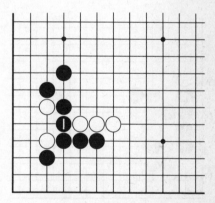

Correct Answer
By playing at 1, all the white stones are linked up into one group.

If Black plays first
If it were Black's turn, he would play 1. Now the two white stones on the left are isolated and cannot make a living shape.

PROBLEM 19

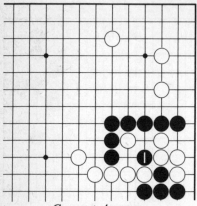

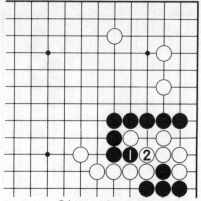

Correct Answer

If Black cuts with 1, there is no way that White can rescue his four stones on the right.

Wrong Answer

If Black plays 1, White connects with 2. All Black can do now is to capture the stone in atari. Black has failed.

PROBLEM 20

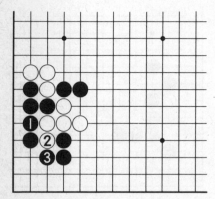

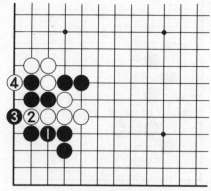

Correct Answer

Black 1 is the correct answer. If White 2, Black plays 3. Black's stones on the bottom left are intact.

Wrong Answer

Black 1 fails. After White 2 and 4, three black stones will be captured.

PROBLEM 21

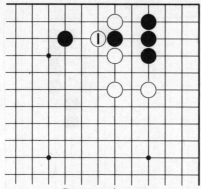

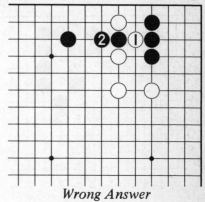

Correct Answer

If White gives atari with 1, his stones above and below will be able to link up.

Wrong Answer

If White gives atari with 1 here, the lone white stone at the top will be cut off and captured after Black 2.

PROBLEM 22

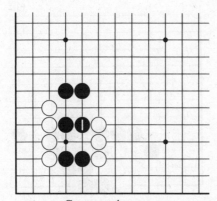

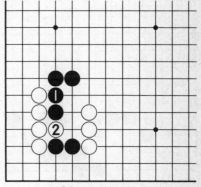

Correct Answer

Black 1 makes a 'bamboo joint'. All the black stones are connected.

Wrong Answer

A move like Black 1 fails. After White 2, the two black stones below are cut off and will die.

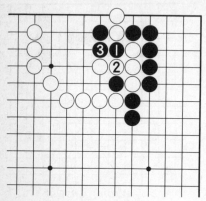

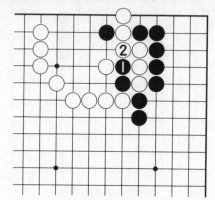

Correct Answer

Black 1 and 3 catch two white stones. White's territory has been devastated.

Wrong Answer

Giving atari with Black 1 fails. White connects with 2 and his position is secure.

PROBLEM 24

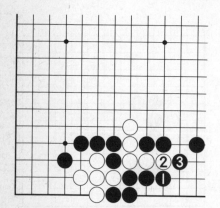

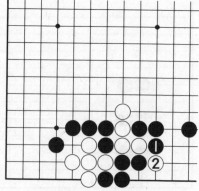

Correct Answer

Black plays 1 and, if White continues with 2, plays 3. All the black stones on the right are now safely connected.

Wrong Answer

Blocking immediately with 1 fails. This lets White catch four stones by giving atari with 2.

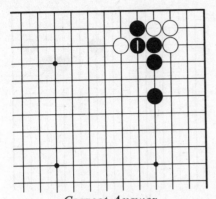

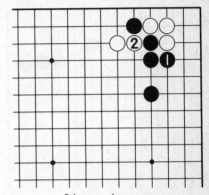

Correct Answer
Black should play 1, thereby linking up all his stones.

Wrong Answer
If White is allowed to play 2, Black's stone at the top will be captured.

PROBLEM 26

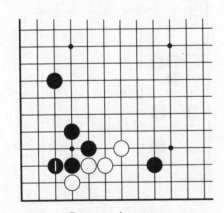

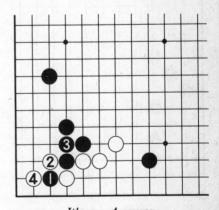

Correct Answer
Black 1 is the correct way to defend his territory against White's intrusion.

Wrong Answer
Black 1 is an overplay. After White 2 and 4, Black suffers a big loss.

PROBLEM 27

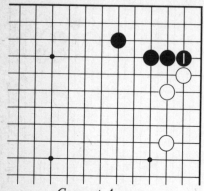

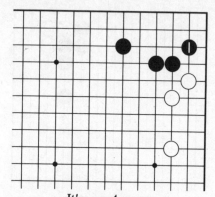

Correct Answer
Black 1 is the correct way for Black to defend his position.

Wrong Answer
All moves other than the correct answer, like Black 1 here, are all inferior and lose points.

PROBLEM 28

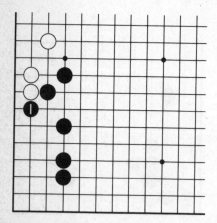

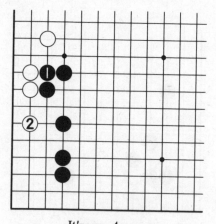

Correct Answer
Black 1 is the correct way for Black to defend his position.

Wrong Answer
If Black makes a move like 1, White will invade with 2, devastating Black's territory.

PROBLEM 29

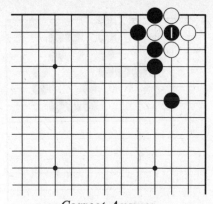

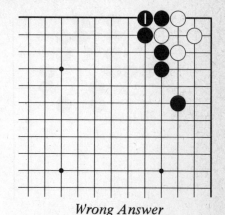

Correct Answer

The only way to play is for Black to take the ko with 1.

Wrong Answer

Connecting with Black 1 is wrong. If he plays this way, White gains the initiative in the ko fight.

PROBLEM 30

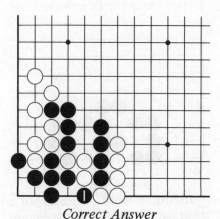

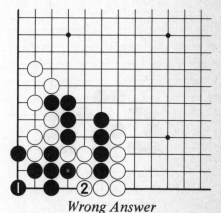

Correct Answer

Starting a ko fight with Black 1 is the only way to rescue the six black stones in the corner.

Wrong Answer

There is no way for Black to make two eyes in the corner. If White plays 2, the black stones are dead.

— 135 —

PROBLEM 31

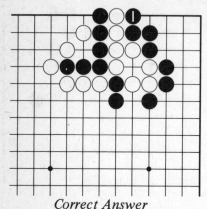

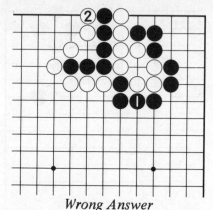

Correct Answer
Giving atari with Black 1 captures all the white stones on the right.

Wrong Answer
Black might be able to capture three white stones with 1, but six black stones die when White gives atari with 2.

PROBLEM 32

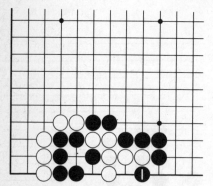

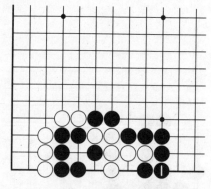

Correct Answer
If Black plays 1, White has no move to save his six stones.

For Reference
In other words, because of a shortage of liberties White cannot give atari to the black stones on the left. But after Black 1, Black can give atari to six white stones from the right.

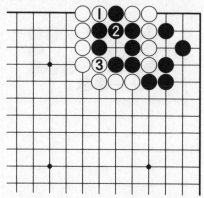

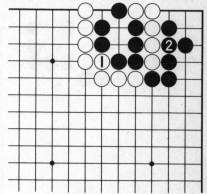

Correct Answer

White 1 forces Black to respond with 2. White 3 then gives atari to the eight black stones.

Wrong Answer

White 1 fails. After giving atari with 2, Black will capture five white stones.

PROBLEM 34

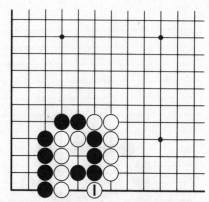

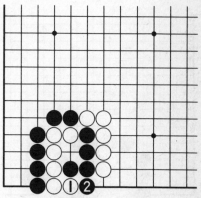

Correct Answer

White 1 catches four black stones. There is no way Black can defend these stones without putting himself into atari.

Wrong Answer

If White plays 1, Black gives atari with 2 and catches six white stones.

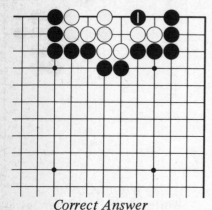

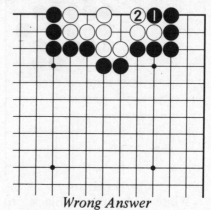

Correct Answer
If Black plays 1, there is no way that White's stones can live.

Wrong Answer
Black 1 here lets White get two eyes and life with 2.

PROBLEM 36

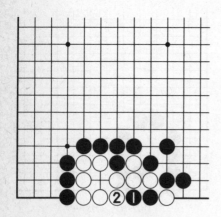

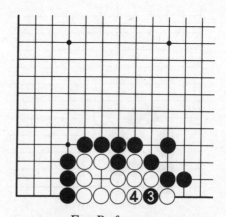

Correct Answer
Sacrificing two stones with 1 is the correct answer. But what does Black do after White 2?

For Reference
Black 3 guarantees that White's eye on the edge will be a false one, so White is dead.

PROBLEM 37

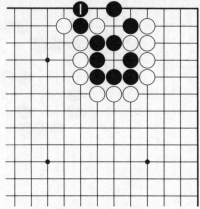

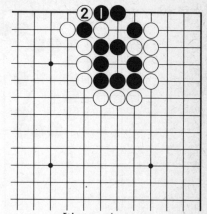

Correct Answer

Not only does Black 1 guarantee the capture of a white stone, it also gives Black two eyes and life.

Wrong Answer

If Black gives atari with 1, White captures a stone with 2. Black has only one eye and is dead.

PROBLEM 38

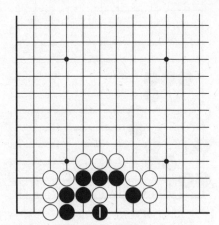

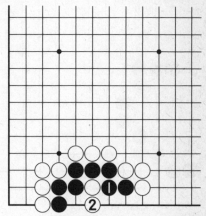

Correct Answer

Black 1 not only catches a white stone but also gives Black two eyes and life.

Wrong Answer

If Black plays 1, White 2 destroys Black's eye shape, so Black is dead.

PROBLEM 39

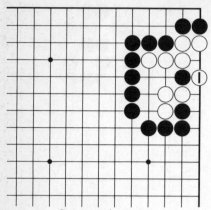 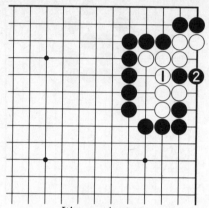

Correct Answer

White 1 not only catches a black stone but also gives White two eyes and life.

Wrong Answer

If White plays 1 from above, Black 2 destroys White's eye shape, so White is dead.

PROBLEM 40

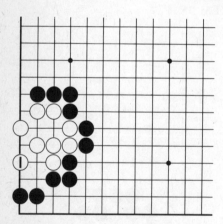 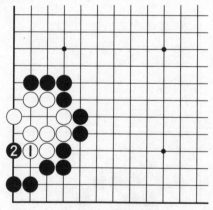

Correct Answer

White can make a second eye by playing at 1, so he is alive.

Wrong Answer

If White plays 1, Black will strike at the vital point with 2. White is now unable to make two eyes, so he is dead.

PROBLEM 41

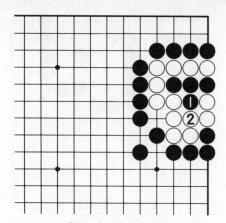

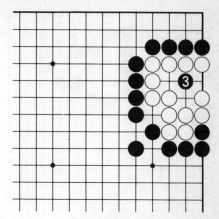

Correct Answer

Sacrificing four stones with Black 1 is the correct answer. If White captures with 2 . . .

For Reference

The shape is now a four-point nakade. After Black 3, White will eventually be reduced to one eye, so he is dead.

PROBLEM 42

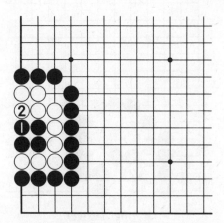

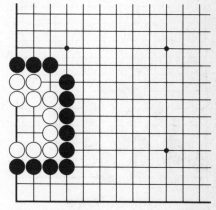

Correct Answer

Sacrificing four stones with Black 1 is the correct answer. If White captures with 2 . . .

For Reference

In this situation White is dead. There is no way he can make two eyes.

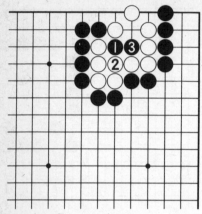

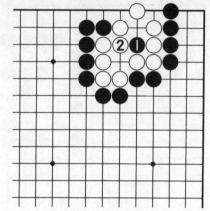

Correct Answer
If Black plays 1 and 3, White dies because he cannot make two eyes.

Wrong Answer
If Black plays 1, White gets two eyes by playing at 2, so he is alive.

PROBLEM 44

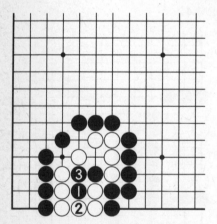

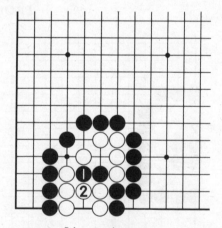

Correct Answer
After the sequence to 3, White must capture three stones, but Black will play back in at the point 3, so White will die.

Wrong Answer
Black 1 fails. After 2, White gets two eyes and lives.

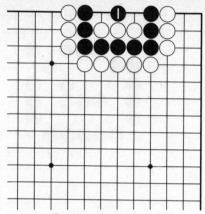

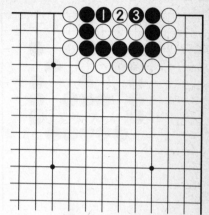

Correct Answer
Black 1 results in a seki.

Wrong Answer
4 played below 2
Black can capture four stones with 1 and 3, but the situation becomes a four-point nakade, so Black is dead.

PROBLEM 46

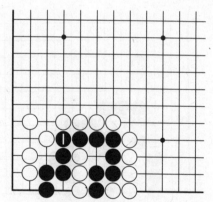

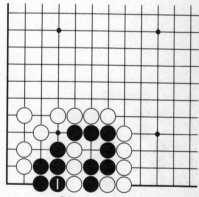

Correct Answer
Black 1 results in a seki.

Wrong Answer
If Black plays 1, he is dead. Even though Black captures three stones, he cannot make two eyes.

PROBLEM 47

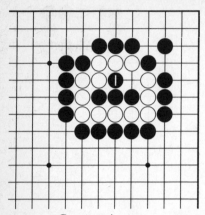

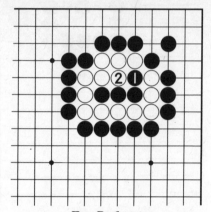

Correct Answer
White is dead. Black will sacrifice four stones by giving atari with 1 and White can only get one eye.

For Reference
Sacrificing four stones with Black 1 here is wrong. After White 2 there is no way to prevent White from making two eyes.

PROBLEM 48

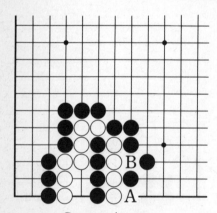

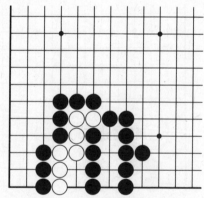

Correct Answer
All the white stones are dead. Black can play at A and B any time he chooses. White cannot try to capture Black.

For Reference
It is easy to see that after Black captures four white stones the seki is broken.

PROBLEM 49

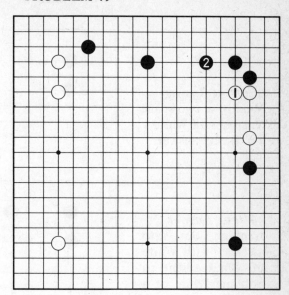

Correct Answer

White must somehow reinforce his position on the right with a move like 1. Black 2 is the normal response.

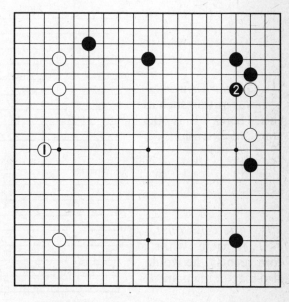

Wrong Answer

If White makes a move in another part of the board, with 1 for example, Black will play 2, putting White at a great disadvantage on the right side.

PROBLEM 50

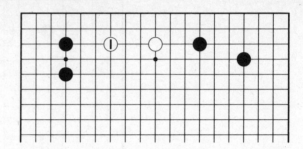

Correct Answer
Making a two-space extension with White 1 is the correct answer.

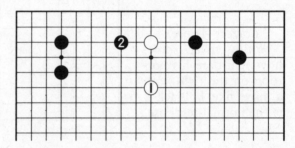

Wrong Answer
Jumping out into the center with White 1 lets Black extend to 2, robbing White of a base along the top.

PROBLEM 51

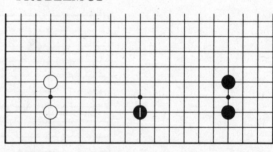

Correct Answer
In a position such as this, Black 1 is the standard extension.

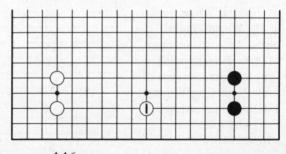

If White Plays First
If it were White's turn to play, he would also play at the point 1.

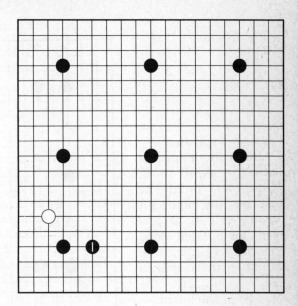

Correct Answer 1
A one-space jump to Black 1 is the standard response to White's move.

Correct Answer 2
Exchanging 1 for 2 before jumping to 3 is also good. Depending on Black's choice of strategy, 3 at A or B is also a good move.

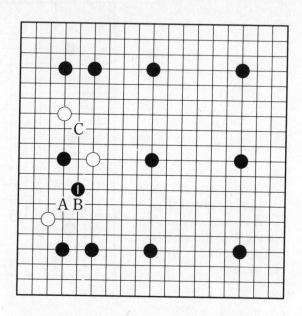

Correct Answer

Black should play at either 1, A, B or C. Whichever point he chooses, the important lesson here is to prevent his isolated stone on the left side from being encircled and to lead it out into the middle of the board.

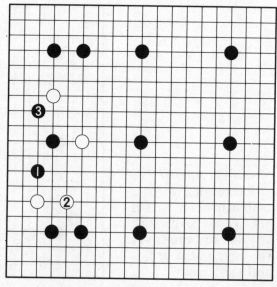

Wrong Answer

It is wrong for Black to try to live immediately with 1 and 3. This kind of play gives Black a small, cramped position on the side, while White builds influence on the outside.

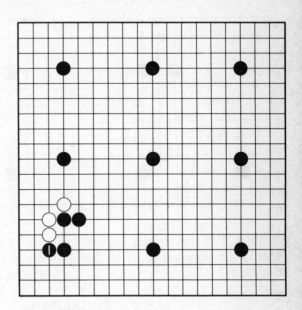

Correct Answer
Blocking White's access to the corner with 1 is the correct response. This move is a basic joseki.

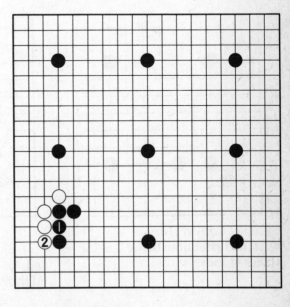

Wrong Answer
Black 1 is a bad move. White moves into the corner with 2. Black has suffered a big loss.

PROBLEM 55

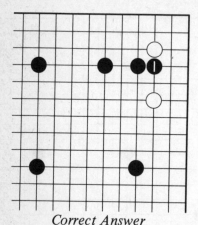

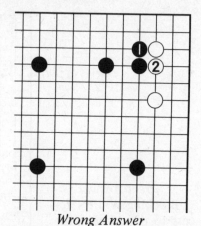

Correct Answer

Black 1 is the correct answer. This is the standard move in this situation.

Wrong Answer

If Black plays 1, White will respond with 2, giving Black an inferior result.

PROBLEM 56

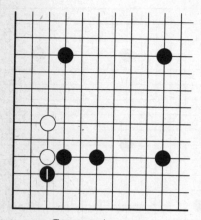

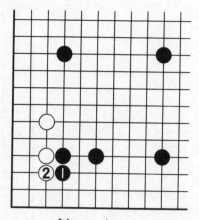

Correct Answer

In this situation Black 1 is the standard move.

Wrong Answer

If Black plays 1, White plays 2 and, as before, Black's result is inferior.

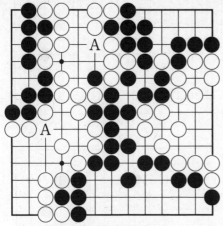

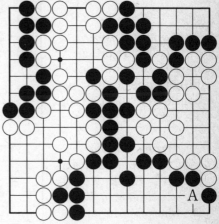

Correct Answer 1

White has two defects: the points A. If Black plays on these points, White will suffer big losses.

Correct Answer 2

Black's defect is at A. If White plays here, Black will suffer a big loss.

PROBLEM 58

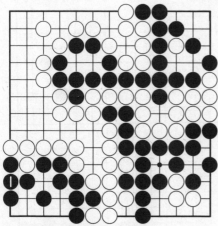

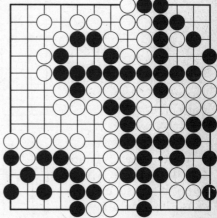

Correct Answer

White's three stones on the left can't live, so Black should fill the ko with 1.

Wrong Answer

Since the three white stones can't live, Black 1 is a wasted move.

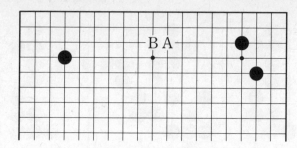

Correct Answer
Invading at either A or B is a good move. Either one could be considered the correct answer.

Wrong Answer
If White were to play C, Black would play 1. If instead White D, Black B. In either case, White would be at a disadvantage. With D, White would suffer an outright loss.

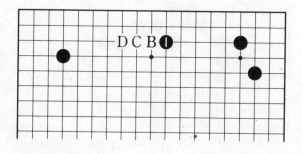

PROBLEM 60

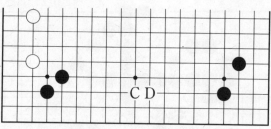

Correct Answer
White C and D are the usual invasion moves. Both are correct.

For Reference
White A and B are too high. White would be a bit insecure because he would be unable to form a safe base. In special positions, however, such moves are conceivable.

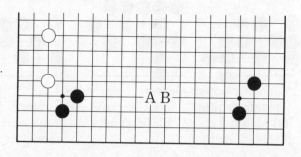

Correct Answer
There is a proverb which says, "Answer the capping move with a knight's move." In conformance with this proverb, Black 1 is the standard response.

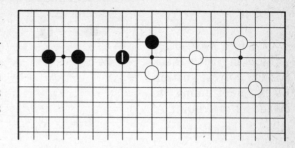

For Reference
Depending on the situation, Black 1 and Black A are also possible responses. Actually, there are many ways of answering the capping move.

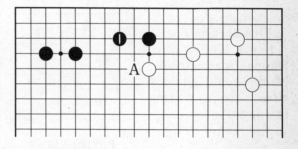

PROBLEM 62

Correct Answer
Blocking with Black 1 here is the correct answer. It is important for Black to make a large territorial framework with his stones on the left. You should block on the wider side.

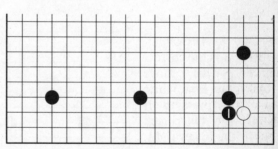

Wrong Answer
Black 1 here allows White to encroach into Black's sphere of influence. Black has suffered a loss.

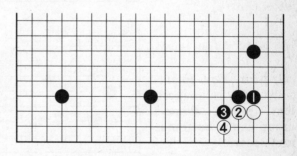

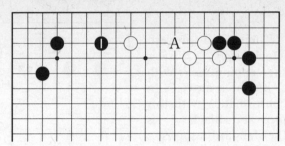

Correct Answer

Blocking with Black 1 is the correct answer. Black next aims to invade at the point A.

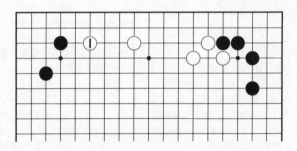

If White Plays First

If it is White's turn, White 1 is a big point. Black should prevent White from playing this move.

PROBLEM 64

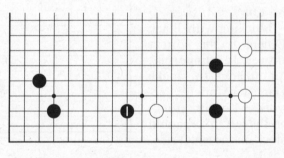

Correct Answer

Black 1 is the correct answer. This move attacks the lone white stone by pressing it against the two black ones in the lower right.

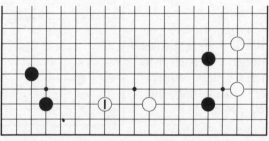

If White Plays First

White 1 is an excellent point. White's group at the bottom is now secure.

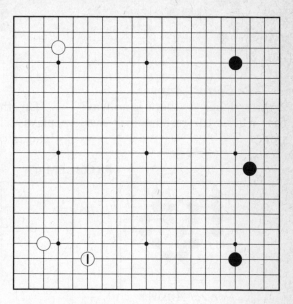

Correct Answer
Making a corner enclosure with 1 is the correct answer. Because of the influence of the black stones on the right, White should aim to make a territorial framework along the left side.

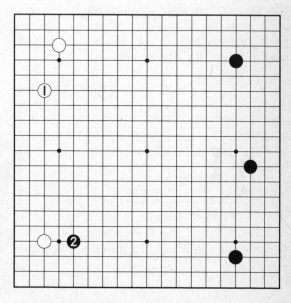

For Reference
If White makes a corner enclosure with 1, Black will play 2. This move works very well in conjunction with Black's stones on the left side to develop a large territorial framework. After Black 2, the game will become difficult for White.

PROBLEM 66

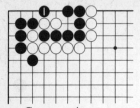

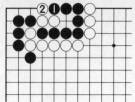

Correct Answer

After Black 1, there is no way for White to rescue his two stones.

Wrong Answer

On the other hand, if Black plays 1 here, White 2 puts eight black stones in atari.

PROBLEM 67

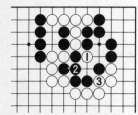

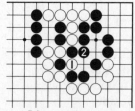

Correct Answer

Giving atari with White 1 is the correct answer. Connecting at 2 is of no help. After White gives atari with 3, Black has no way to rescue his five stones.

Wrong Answer

Capturing a stone with 1 fails. After Black connects with 2, the six white stones at the top will die.

PROBLEM 68

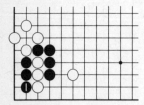

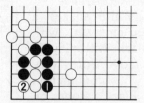

Correct Answer

After Black 1, the three white stones can't avoid being captured.

Wrong Answer

If Black presses from the outside with 1 here, White 2 will catch the two black stones in the corner.

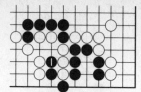

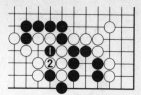

Correct Answer

If Black gives atari to three white stones with 1, there is no way that White can save them. Thus, Black can connect his stones at the bottom to the ones on the outside.

Wrong Answer

Giving atari with Black 1 here, leads to the loss of eight black stones at the bottom.

PROBLEM 70

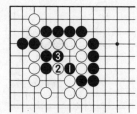

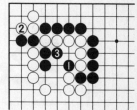

Correct Answer

The combination of 1 and 3 leads to a snapback, so the six white stones will be captured.

For Reference

If White responds to Black 1 with 2, Black gives atari with 3 and wins the capturing race. Black 1 is the only move that will capture the six white stones.

PROBLEM 71

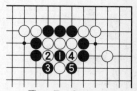

Correct Answer

Black 1 is the key move. White might struggle to escape with 2 and 4, but after Black 5 White can't escape.

For Reference

White 2 and 4 are symmetrical to the correct answer moves, but the result is the same. This shape is known as 'the crane's nest'.

PROBLEM 72

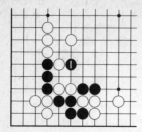

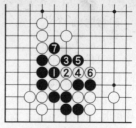

Correct Answer
Black 1 is the key move to capture two stones. All the black stones are now connected.

Wrong Answer
The sequence from Black 1 to 7 is too blunt. Even though some of Black's stones have escaped, the rest are dead.

PROBLEM 73

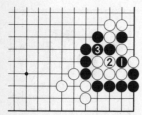

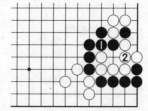

Correct Answer
Sacrificing a stone with 1 and then giving atari with 3 traps five white stones.

Wrong Answer
Black 1 here fails. White saves all of his stones by connecting at 2.

PROBLEM 74

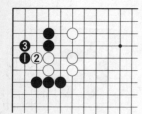

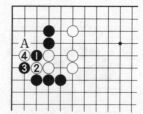

Correct Answer
Black 1 is the vital point for linking up the two black groups. There is no way White can break the connection.

Wrong Answer
Black 1 and 3 are refuted by White 2 and 4. If Black plays 1 at A, White 2 at 4 again leads to Black's failure.

PROBLEM 75

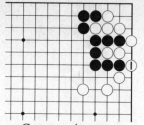

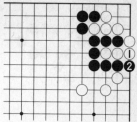

Correct Answer

White 1 establishes the link. If Black takes two white stones, White retakes one stone.

Wrong Answer

If White tries to save his two stones in atari with 1, Black gives atari with 2 and the white group in the corner is dead.

PROBLEM 76

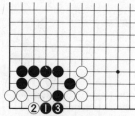

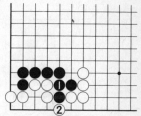

Correct Answer

Black 1 prevents White from linking up his two groups. After Black 3, the white stones in the corner are dead.

Wrong Answer

1 may seem like a weak point, but if Black reinforces here, White links up all his stones with 2.

PROBLEM 77

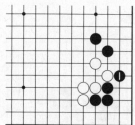

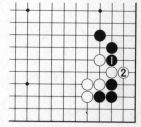

Correct Answer

Black 1 is a simple move, but it secures a connection between the top and bottom black groups.

Wrong Answer

Black 1 here fails. After White 2, Black is unable to connect his two groups.

PROBLEM 78

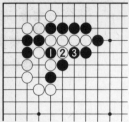

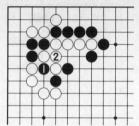

Correct Answer

Sacrificing a stone with Black 1 is a brilliant move. Black 3 next makes escape impossible.

Wrong Answer

Black 1 here has no meaning. If White is able to connect at the point 2, there is no way to capture the white stones.

PROBLEM 79

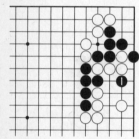

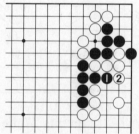

Correct Answer

If Black plays 1, it will be impossible for the four white stones to escape.

Wrong Answer

Black 1 is a crass move. White can escape with 2. Now the black stones in the corner are dead.

PROBLEM 80

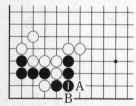

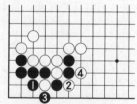

Correct Answer

Either Black 1 or A is the correct answer. Playing at B is a bit inferior, however.

Wrong Answer

Black 1 here is a mistake. Black loses two stones when White plays 2 and 4.

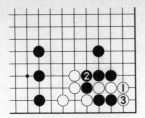

Correct Answer

White 1 is the right move. Now when Black plays 2, White can take two stones with 3.

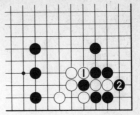

Wrong Answer

White 1 is the move you learn when studying joseki, but here it is inferior to the correct answer.

PROBLEM 82

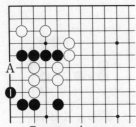

Correct Answer

Either Black 1 or A will ensure a connection between the two black groups.

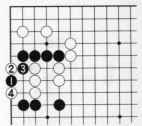

Wrong Answer

Black 1 here fails. White 2 and 4 prevent Black from linking up his groups.

PROBLEM 83

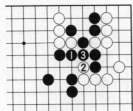

Correct Answer

Black 1 is the only move that keeps all of Black's stones connected. If White tries to separate them with 2, Black connects with 3.

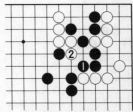

Wrong Answer

Black 1 fails. White plays 2, aiming to cut the black stones in two places.

PROBLEM 84

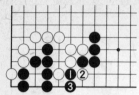 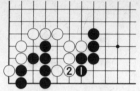

Correct Answer
Black 1 is the vital point. If White plays 2, Black plays 3 and there is no way that White can prevent Black from linking up.

Wrong Answer
Any other move, like Black 1, for instance, fails. After White 2, it is impossible for Black to link up his groups, so the corner dies.

PROBLEM 85

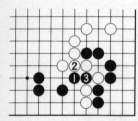 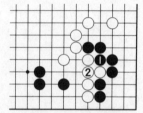

Correct Answer
Black 1 aims at two cutting points, 2 and 3. Whichever one White defends, Black will cut at the other.

Wrong Answer
Black 1 is a bad move because it forces White to defend one of his weak points. Now all the white stones are connected.

PROBLEM 86

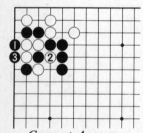 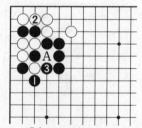

Correct Answer
Black 1 and 3 put three white stones in atari. White cannot escape. Reversing the order of 1 and 3 is also correct.

Wrong Answer
Capturing a stone with 1 and 3 is bad because Black loses two stones when White plays 2. Black 1 at A is even worse.

PROBLEM 87

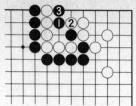

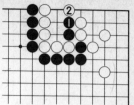

Correct Answer

Black 1 and 3 set up a snap-back, so Black can capture six white stones.

Wrong Answer

If Black plays 1, he will lose two stones when White plays 2. This is a failure for Black.

PROBLEM 88

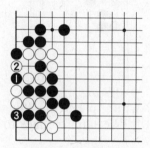

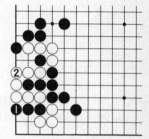

Correct Answer

The trick is to sacrifice a stone with Black 1. After White 2, Black gives atari with 3 and White can't connect at 1 because of a shortage of liberties.

Wrong Answer

Black 1 is too simple. White connects at 2 and Black is at a loss for a follow-up move. Black has failed.

PROBLEM 89

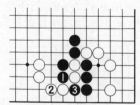

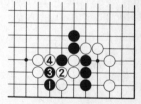

Correct Answer

If Black gives atari with 1, all White can do is to extend to 2. If White 2 at 3, Black 3 at 2 and Black captures four stones.

Wrong Answer

Black 1 is an overplay. Black suffers a big loss with the sequence to White 4.

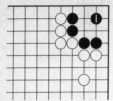

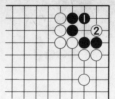

Correct Answer
Black 1 is good 'shape' and the black stones are now alive.

Wrong Answer
If Black plays any other move, he will be at a disadvantage.

PROBLEM 91

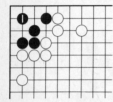

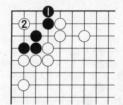

Correct Answer
Black 1 is the point to make a living shape for the black group.

Wrong Answer
If White plays on this vital point, it'll be hard for Black to live.

PROBLEM 92

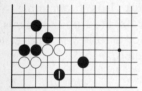

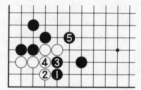

Correct Answer
Black 1 is the vital point for attacking the white group.

For Reference
If White defends with 2 and 4, White is dead after Black 5.

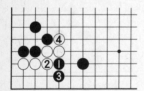

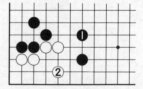

Wrong Answer 1
Black 1 and 3 are 'gote', so White can escape with 4.

Wrong Answer 2
Black 1 lacks forcefulness. White can easily live with 2.

PROBLEM 93

Correct Answer
Jumping out into the center with Black 1 is the standard way to play in this type of position. Next, if White A, Black will play B.

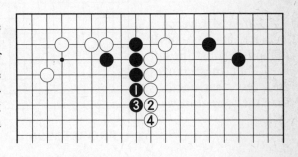

Wrong Answer
Black 1 and 3 are answered by White 2 and 4. This way of moving out into the center is often disadvantageous for Black because White keeps a step ahead.

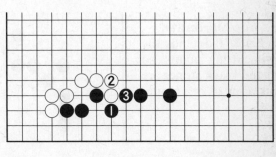

PROBLEM 94

Correct Answer
Black should play at 1. If White 2, Black 3. In this way he can link up his two groups on the left and right.

Wrong Answer
Cutting at 1 is unreasonable for Black. After White 2 and 4, Black is in trouble.

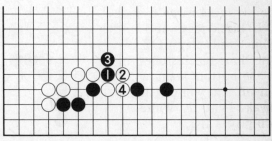

PROBLEM 95

Correct Answer
It is imperative that Black defend the cut (to the right of 1) with 1. This move is essential if Black is going to make a moyo on the left.

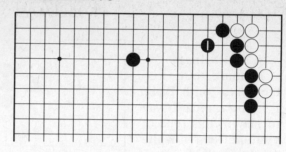

Wrong Answer
Black at 1, A or B defends against the cut at 1, but these moves are less satisfactory than the correct answer.

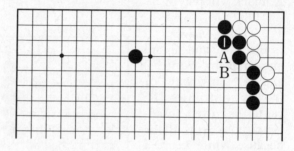

PROBLEM 96

Correct Answer
Black 1 defends the two cutting points, so all the black stones are linked up as one group.

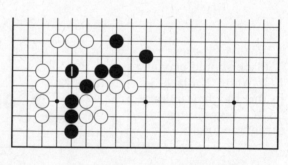

Wrong Answer
If Black plays at 1, White will play at 2. The three black stones at the bottom are now cut off and will die. If Black 1 at 2, White will play 2 at 1.

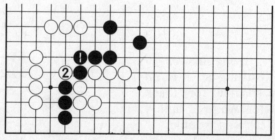

Correct Answer

'Play at the head of two stones.' Following this proverb, Black 1 is the vital point.

Wrong Answer

Black 1 is also at the 'head of two stones', but in this case it is unsatisfactory since White can take the strategic point of 4.

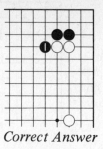

Correct Answer

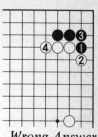

Wrong Answer

Unsatisfactory

Black 1 here lacks the power of the correct answer. Black's result is unsatisfactory.

If White Plays First

If it were White's turn, he would play at 1, his vital point, which is 'the head of two stones'.

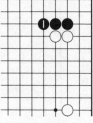

Unsatisfactory

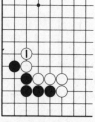
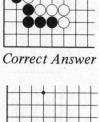

If White Plays First

Correct Answer

The correct shape in this position is for White to extend to 1. This is the only move.

For Reference

After White 1, Black exchanges 2 for 3 and the position will be left as it is for the time being.

Correct Answer

For Reference

Wrong Answer 1

White 1 is unreasonable. Black 2 and 4 capture a stone and White has suffered a big loss.

Wrong Answer 2

White 1 may look like good shape, but Black can easily move out along the side with 2. White's result is inferior.

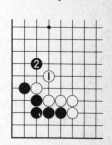

Wrong Answer 1

Wrong Answer 2

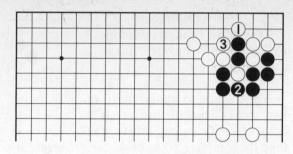

Correct Answer
White 1 is the vital point. When Black takes with 2, White can easily link up his two groups with 3.

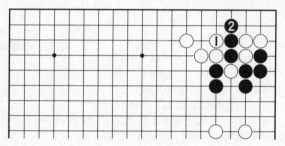

Wrong Answer
If White gives atari with 1, Black will play 2 and the three white stones in the corner will die.

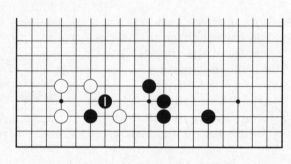

Correct Answer
Black should move out with 1. If White tries to save his isolated stone, he will have a very difficult fight.

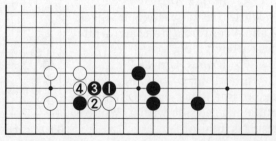

Wrong Answer
Black 1 here is an overplay. White counterattacks with 2 and 4, catching a black stone.

Correct Answer
Black has no choice but to sacrifice one stone by giving atari with 1. When White captures with 2, Black gives atari to two stones with 3.

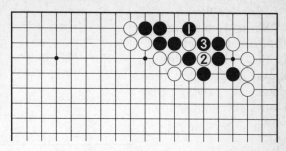

Wrong Answer
If Black connects with 1, White plays 2 and 4, catching four black stones. In addition, the remaining seven black stones are insecure because they lack 'eye shape'.

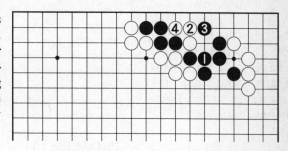

PROBLEM 102

Correct Answer
Black 1 strikes at the weak point of White's shape. With the sequence to 5, White has suffered a big loss.

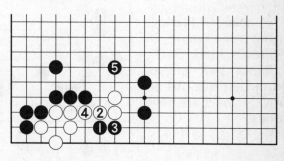

Wrong Answer
If Black plays 1, White's stones are secure after 2. If Black 1 at A, White 2 at B. In either case, Black has failed.

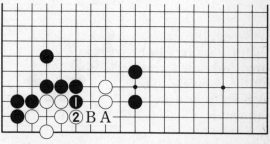

PROBLEM 103

Correct Answer
White 1, playing 'at the head of two stones', is the correct fighting move. If Black 2, White plays 3, giving his stones excellent shape.

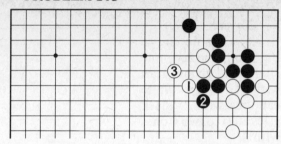

Wrong Answer
White 1 allows Black to take the vital point of 2. After the exchange of 3 for 4, it is Black who has the advantage in the fighting to follow.

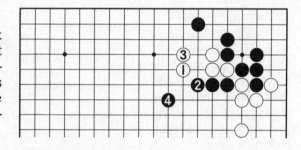

PROBLEM 104

Correct Answer
Jumping to Black 1 is the correct move. If White 2, Black 3 establishes the linkup on the left side. All of Black's stones are now strong.

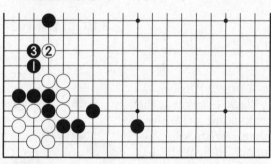

Wrong Answer
Black 1 is a very bad move. White forces with the sequence to 6 and Black is at a great disadvantage.

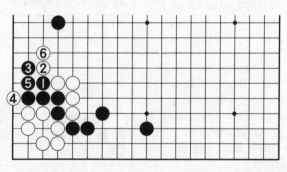

PROBLEM 105

Correct Answer
Black 1 and 3 are the moves that secure the corner for Black. At this point, play in this part of the board comes to a pause.

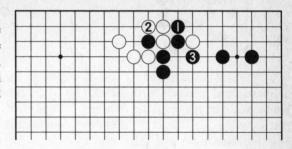

Wrong Answer
Black 1 is unreasonable. After White 2, not only are Black's stones on the left dead but his territory on the right is devastated. Black 1 at A is also bad.

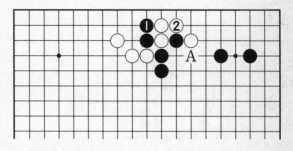

PROBLEM 106

Correct Answer
1 gives Black good shape. After White extends to 2, the sequence comes to an end. Black 1 and White 2 in this exchange are standard moves.

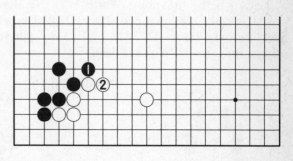

Wrong Answer
Not only is Black 1 gote, but it also gives him bad shape. White can now play elsewhere or, if he wants, can play a good move at A.

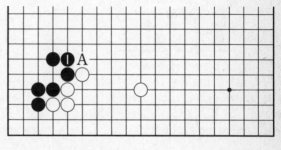

PROBLEM 107

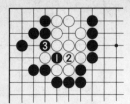

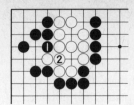

Correct Answer
Sacrificing a stone with Black 1 is a brilliant move. After White takes with 2, Black 3 makes White's second eye a false one.

Wrong Answer
If Black first plays 1, White makes a second real eye at 2, giving his group life.

PROBLEM 108

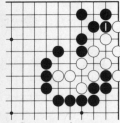

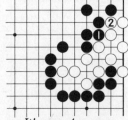

Correct Answer
Black 1 is the vital point. White now has only one real eye (two lines below Black 1). All the others are false, so White is dead.

Wrong Answer
If Black plays anywhere else, White will make his second eye by playing at 2, giving him life.

PROBLEM 109

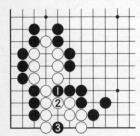

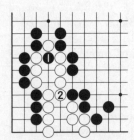

Correct Answer
Black 1 makes the big white eye above false, then after White plays 2, Black 3 leaves White with only one real eye.

Wrong Answer
If White is allowed to play at 2, Black will be unable to prevent White from making two eyes below.

PROBLEM 110

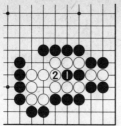

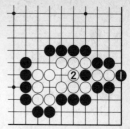

Correct Answer

Black must sacrifice two stones with 1, then after White takes with 2, throw in another stone to the right of 1. White is dead because he has only one eye.

Wrong Answer

Even though you can capture two stones with Black 1, White is able to play at 2, giving him two eyes and life.

PROBLEM 111

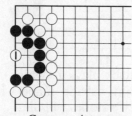

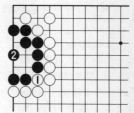

Correct Answer

White 1 is the vital point of the 5-point nakade shape. Black will eventually be reduced to one eye and so he is dead.

Wrong Answer

If you let Black occupy the vital point of 2, there is no way to kill his stones.

PROBLEM 112

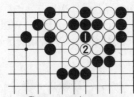

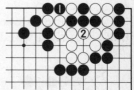

Correct Answer

Black must increase his sacrifice to five stones by playing at 1. After White captures with 2, Black destroys White's eye shape by playing 3 one point above 1.

Wrong Answer

If Black captures a stone at 1, White 2 puts four black stones into atari. Black can't escape, so White can now live.

PROBLEM 113

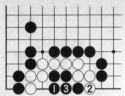

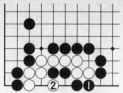

Correct Answer

Black 1 and 3 create a 5-point nakade shape. White is dead.

Wrong Answer

If Black 1, White 2 catches two stones. White gets two eyes.

PROBLEM 114

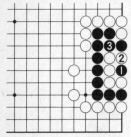

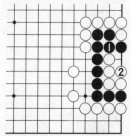

Correct Answer

Black 1 prevents White from making a 5-point nakade shape. If White 2, Black lives with 3.

Wrong Answer

If Black plays 1, White makes a 5-point nakade shape with 2, so Black's stones will die.

PROBLEM 115

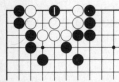

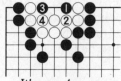

Correct Answer

Black 1 threatens two snap-backs. Two white stones on either the left or right will die.

Wrong Answer

Giving atari with 1 and 3 just lets White live. After White 4, Black can't destroy White's eyes.

PROBLEM 116

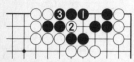

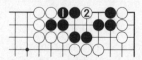

Correct Answer

Black 1 is the vital point for eye shape. If White 2, Black lives with 3 and vice versa.

Wrong Answer

If Black plays at 1, White gives atari with 2. Black is dead.

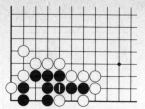

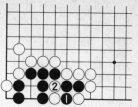

Correct Answer

If Black connects at 1, there is no way for the isolated white stone to escape. So Black has two eyes and is alive.

Wrong Answer

If Black plays 1, he puts himself into atari and is captured by White on the next move. All the black stones are now dead.

PROBLEM 118

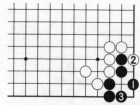

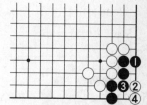

Correct Answer

Black 1 is the vital point. If White 2, Black 3 makes two eyes. If White 2 at 3, Black 3 at 2 again makes two eyes.

Wrong Answer

If Black plays 1, White hits the vital point with 2. After White 4, Black will eventually be reduced to a 3-point nakade, so he is dead.

PROBLEM 119

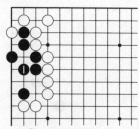

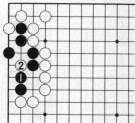

Correct Answer

If Black plays at 1, he will have no trouble making a second eye.

Wrong Answer

If Black plays 1, he is killed by White 2. Black 1 in the correct answer is the only way to live.

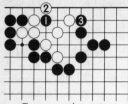

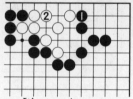

Correct Answer
Black 1 destroys White's eye shape. If White 2, Black 3 kills all the white stones.

Wrong Answer
Timing is important. If Black 1 first, White gets two eyes by playing at the vital point of 2.

PROBLEM 121

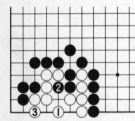

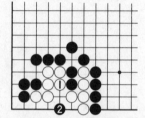

Correct Answer
If White plays 1, he can make his second eye at either 2 or 3. That is, if Black plays one of these points, White will play the other.

Wrong Answer
If White 1, the killing move is Black 2. Even though White can capture two stones, his group still only has one eye.

PROBLEM 122

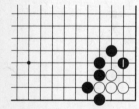

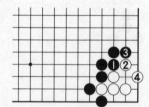

Correct Answer
Black 1 is on the point where White wants to make his second eye, so White is dead.

Wrong Answer
If White is allowed to play at 2, he cannot be killed.

Correct Answer
Taking with Black 1 is a huge move. It gives Black certain profit and thickness in the lower left corner. In the meantime, White has used two moves in the lower right corner, but Black can easily live with 3. 1 is a timely move that gives Black a solid lead.

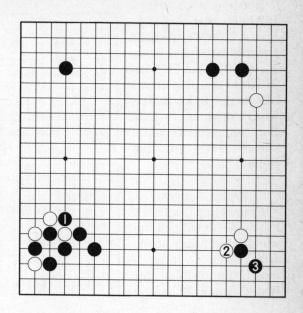

For Reference
If Black responds in the lower right corner with 1, White takes the ko with 2, and Black doesn't have a ko threat. There is a proverb that says: "There are no ko threats in the beginning of the game." Black's position here is inferior to the one in the correct answer diagram.

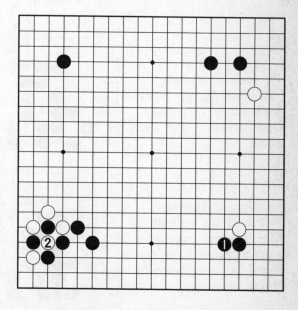

Correct Answer

Starting a ko with 1 is White's best chance to live. It gives White a light and resilient shape. When Black takes the ko with 2, White can play moves like A and B, ko threats which threaten to lead the endangered white stones out into the center.

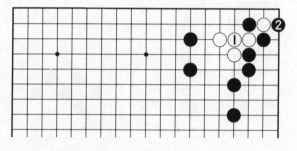

Wrong Answer

Connecting with 1 leaves White with an unwieldy and heavy shape after Black 2. It is almost impossible for White's stones to live.

PROBLEM 125

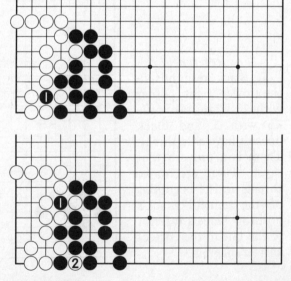

Correct Answer

Taking the ko below with Black 1 is bigger than taking the ko above.

Wrong Answer

Taking the ko with 1 here is worth less than a half a point. The ko below, however, is worth almost 2 points.

PROBLEM 126

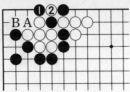

Correct Answer

Starting a ko with Black 1 is the correct answer. If White 2 at A, Black plays B, and it is still a ko.

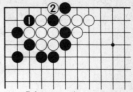

Wrong Answer

Black 1 is a bad move. After White captures a stone with 2, all of White's stones are settled.

PROBLEM 127

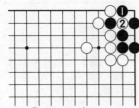

Correct Answer

The only way Black can live in the corner is to create a ko with 1. White 2 starts the ko fight.

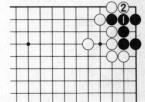

Wrong Answer

If Black connects at 1, White destroys Black's second eye with 2. Black is unconditionally dead.

PROBLEM 128

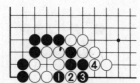

Correct Answer

Black 1, followed by 3, is the correct way to start the ko fight. After White 4, Black takes the ko by playing 5 at 1.

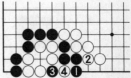

Wrong Answer

Reversing the order of moves with 1 and 3 here is disadvantageous for Black. After White 4, Black must look for a ko threat instead of taking the ko.

PROBLEM 129

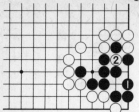

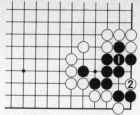

Correct Answer
Black should play 1. The life of the black group now depends on which side wins the ko after White 2.

Wrong Answer
Connecting the ko with 1 lets White destroy Black's eye shape with 2. Black is dead.

PROBLEM 130

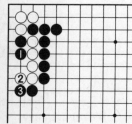

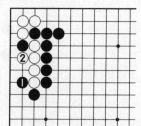

Correct Answer
Black 1 is the vital point. If White 2, Black 3. Black wins the capturing race by one move.

Wrong Answer
Black 1 lets White capture a black stone with 2. The white stones are now safe.

PROBLEM 131

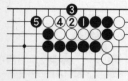

Correct Answer
Black 1 is the vital point. Up to 5, it is easy to see that Black wins the capturing race by one move. If White 2 at 4, Black plays 3 at 5.

Wrong Answer
If Black plays 1, White captures three stones with 2 and 4. Black has failed.

PROBLEM 132

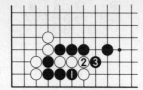

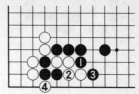

Correct Answer
Black 1 is the vital point. If White 2, Black 3. There is no way that White can save his four stones.

Wrong Answer
Black 1 and 3 are bad moves. White captures three stones with 2 and 4.

PROBLEM 133

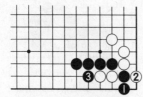

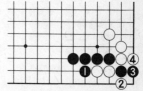

Correct Answer
Black 1 is the vital point. After Black 3, White cannot attack the two black stones in the corner because of his shortage of liberties.

Wrong Answer
Any other move, like Black 1, will fail. White gives atari at the vital point with 2 and catches two black stones.

PROBLEM 134

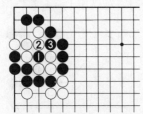

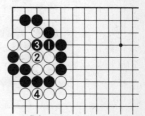

Correct Answer
Black 1, followed by 3, is the correct sacrifice tactic. If White connects at 1 with 4, he loses the capturing race by one move.

Wrong Answer
Without the sacrifice, Black loses the capturing race, as can be seen from the sequence to White 4.

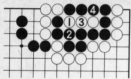

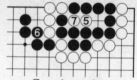

Correct Answer

Giving atari with 1 and then extending to 3, sacrificing three stones, is the correct answer. After Black takes three stones with 4 —

Continuation

The position is now a 3-point nakade. White 5 and 7 win the capturing race by one move.

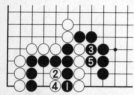

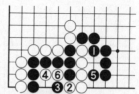

Correct Answer

Black 1 is correct. Black now easily wins the capturing race with 3 and 5.

Wrong Answer

If Black plays 1 here first, White exchanges 2 for Black 3 and Black loses the capturing race.

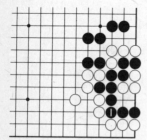

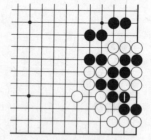

Correct Answer

Black 1 is the vital point If White 2, the position is a 4-point nakade, so Black has five liberties to White's four.

Wrong Answer

Black 1 here makes it just a 3-point nakade. In this case, Black loses the capturing race by two moves.

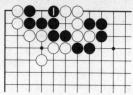

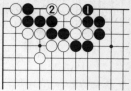

Correct Answer

Black 1, making an eye, is the vital point. White has no way to attack, so Black has won the fight.

Wrong Answer

If Black plays 1, White will play on the vital point of 2. The position is now a seki.

PROBLEM 139

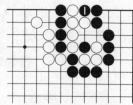

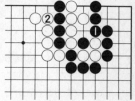

Correct Answer

Black must give atari to the pivotal white stones with 1. This move guarantees the capture of all eight white stones.

Wrong Answer

If Black captures three stones with 1, White gives atari with 2, catching the four black stones to the left.

PROBLEM 140

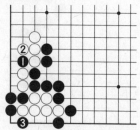

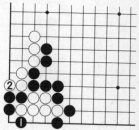

Correct Answer

Sacrificing a stone with Black 1 is the vital point. After 3, Black wins the capturing race by one move.

Wrong Answer

Playing at Black 1 first, allows White to play directly at 2 (in the correct answer White can't play here). Black has failed.

PROBLEM 141

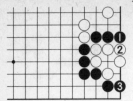

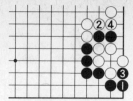

Correct Answer

Black 1, followed by 3, is the correct order of moves. After this, Black wins the capturing race by one move.

Wrong Answer

Black 1 here fails. White 2 and 4 capture two black stones.

PROBLEM 142

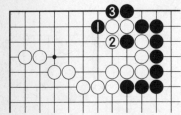

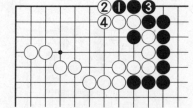

Correct Answer

Attaching at 1 is a brilliant move. After Black 3, White's territory is devastated. If White 2 at 3, Black 3 at 2.

Wrong Answer

Black 1 makes only a small dent in White's territory. The correct answer is more than 10 points better.

PROBLEM 143

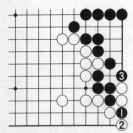

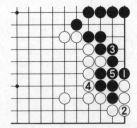

Correct Answer

Black should sacrifice a stone with 1 and then play atari with 3. White can't connect, so Black will capture two stones.

Wrong Answer

Giving atari with 1 immediately is bad. If you compare the result to 5 with the correct answer, you will see that Black has suffered a big loss.

PROBLEM 144

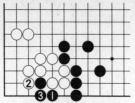

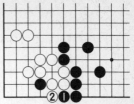

Correct Answer

By linking up his isolated stone on the left to the stones on the right with 1 and 3, Black can make a big intrusion into White's territory.

Wrong Answer

Black 1 is a bad move. Compared to the correct answer, Black has suffered a big loss.

PROBLEM 145

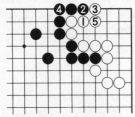

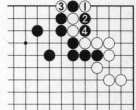

Correct Answer

Because White's two stones to the left are short of liberties, White must passively play 1.

Wrong Answer

If White plays 1 here, Black cuts with 2 and White's territory is greatly reduced in size.

PROBLEM 146

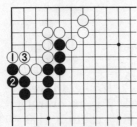

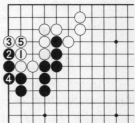

Correct Answer

Since White's two stones at the bottom left have an extra liberty, in the case White can give an atari at 1.

Wrong Answer

White 1 in this position is uncalled for. The result to 5 is two points less for White than the correct answer.

PROBLEM 147

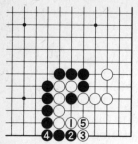

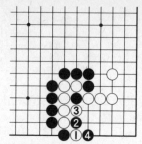

Correct Answer

Because White's five stones are short of liberties, White must passively draw back to 1.

Wrong Answer

If White gives atari with 1, Black cuts with 2. White 3 is forced, and after 4 Black has made a big intrusion into White's territory.

PROBLEM 148

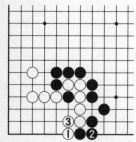

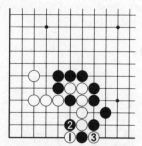

Correct Answer

In this case, White's five stones have an extra liberty on the outside, so White can aggressively give atari at 1. In response, all Black can do is to connect at 2.

Wrong Answer

Black 2 is an overplay. White can safely capture at 3 — Black has no follow-up move.

Correct Answer
Black 1 and 3 are sente moves which are worth 4 points in total. This is much bigger than capturing the lone white stone on the left.

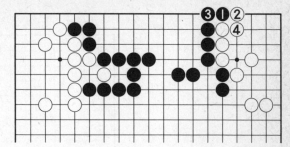

Wrong Answer
Catching the white stone with Black 1 is worth only 3 points in gote. White can now play 2 and 4 on the right, reducing Black's territory by 2 points and expanding his own by 2 points (4 points in total).

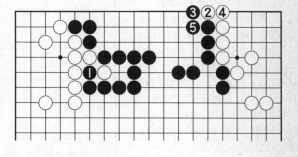

PROBLEM 150

Correct Answer
Black 1 and 3 are worth 2 points in gote. These moves are bigger than playing in the lower left corner.

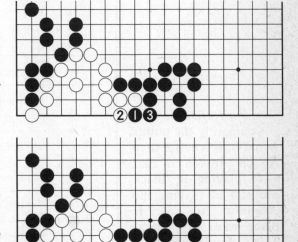

Wrong Answer
Black 1 is worth only 1 point in gote. White 2 and 4 are 1 point bigger, so Black has suffered a loss.

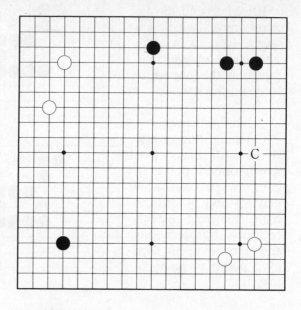

Correct Answer
When two corner en-
closures face each other,
the midpoint between
them is usually the big-
gest point. Therefore,
of the three choices in
the problem, Black at C
is the best point to play.

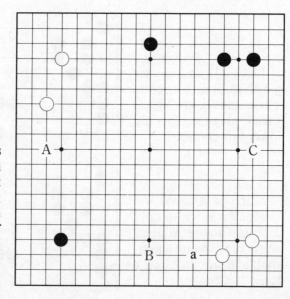

For Reference
Comparing the points
A and B, B is better than
A. The reason is that
after playing B, Black
can aim at playing the
extension to 'a'. If
Black were to play at
A, he would not have
a good follow-up move.

Correct Answer
The diagonal move of Black 1 is the correct answer. This move both defends the corner and attacks the two white stones along the side.

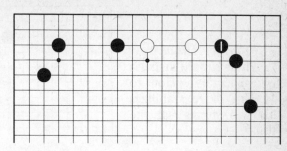

Wrong Answer
Although Black 1 here strongly defends the corner, it doesn't put much pressure on White's position along the side.

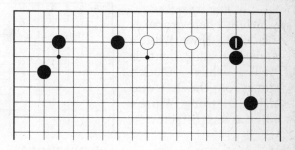

PROBLEM 153

Correct Answer
In this shape, Black 1 is the usual move. Black A is also correct.

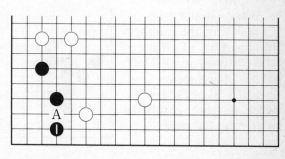

For Reference
Black 1 is overly defensive. It loses territory, so Black is a bit dissatisfied. In special cases, Black A or B may be a good move.

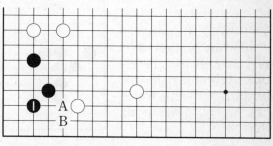

PROBLEM 154

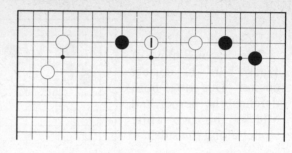

Correct Answer
White should make a two-space extension to 1. This move stabilizes his two stones at the top.

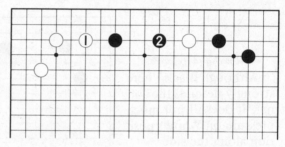

Wrong Answer
White 1 here provokes Black 2. Now White's stone on the right is weak while Black's stones on the left and right are strong. White's result is unsatisfactory.

PROBLEM 155

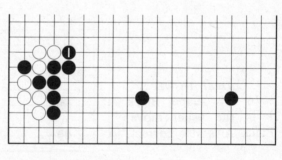

Correct Answer
Black should turn at 1, reducing the number of liberties of White's three stones to the left of 1. This move also expands Black's framework on the right. This is an essential move.

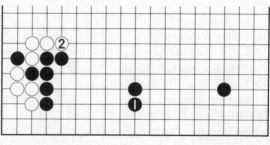

Wrong Answer
If White is allowed to play at 2, Black's development on the right will be restricted while White can freely develop at the top.

Correct Answer
Black must play at 1. Not only is this a big move territorially, but, most important, it also attacks the two white stones.

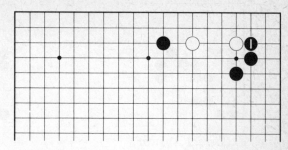

Wrong Answer
Black 1 is bad. White slides into the corner with 2, stabilizing his stones. Black has lost both territory and a target to attack.

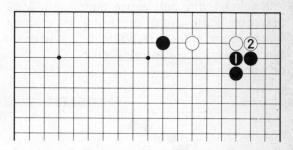

PROBLEM 157

Correct Answer
Jumping out to 1 is the vital point. This move makes Black's two stones strong and leaves White with two weak groups.

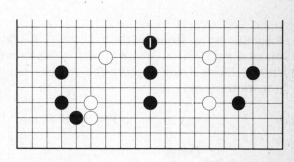

Wrong Answer
Defending the left side with 1 lets White cap with 2, severely attacking the two black stones in the center. Black should be unhappy with this result.

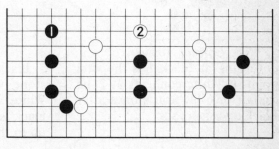

PROBLEM 158

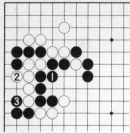

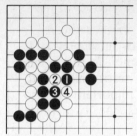

Correct Answer
Black 1 is the only move that prevents White from capturing Black's four stones. If White 2, Black 3 wins the capturing race on the left side.

Wrong Answer
Black 1 fails. White sacrifices a stone with 2 and traps Black with the atari of 4.

PROBLEM 159

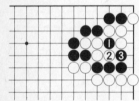

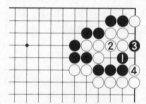

Correct Answer
Sacrificing a stone with 1 is the vital point. After White takes with 2, Black 3 will capture the four white stones.

Wrong Answer
Black 1 and 3 fail. After 4, White wins the capturing race by one move.

PROBLEM 160

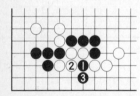

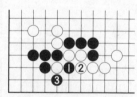

Correct Answer
Cutting at Black 1 is the vital point. If White connects at 2, he cannot save his four stones after Black descends to 3.

Wrong Answer
Black is able to capture one stone with 1 and 3, but when White connects at 2, the four black stones above cannot link up to the ones below.

PROBLEM 161

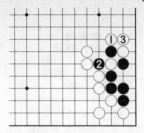

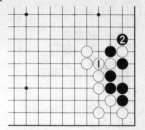

Correct Answer
If White sacrifices a stone by playing 1 and 3, the black stones will die.

Wrong Answer
If White connects at 1, Black will capture a stone with 2. White has suffered a big loss.

PROBLEM 162

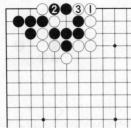

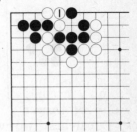

Correct Answer
White 1 is the vital point. After White 3, there is no way Black can rescue his five endangered stones.

Wrong Answer
If White connects at 1, Black can capture the three white stones any time he chooses.

PROBLEM 163

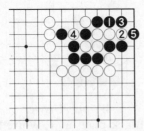

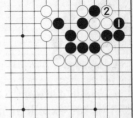

Correct Answer
The sequence to Black 5 catches the four white stones in question.

Wrong Answer
Exchanging Black 1 for White 2 is bad. All the black stones are now dead.

PROBLEM 164

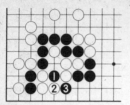

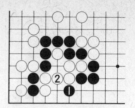

Correct Answer
Black 1 and 3 can capture four white stones in a snapback. If White 2 at 3, Black plays 3 at 2.

Wrong Answer
Black 1 allows White to connect at 2. It is now impossible to capture the white stones, so seven black ones will die.

PROBLEM 165

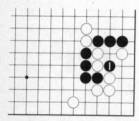

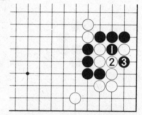

Correct Answer
Black 1 catches two white stones. The two black groups are now linked up.

Wrong Answer
Although Black 1 and 3 capture a stone, Black ends up with four stones drifting without eyes in the center of the board.

PROBLEM 166

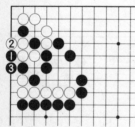

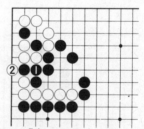

Correct Answer
Black 1 is an excellent move. If White 2, Black can play at 3 and because of a shortage of liberties, White can't give atari. So the six white stones below are dead.

Wrong Answer
If Black plays at 1, White links up underneath with 2. If Black 1 at 2, White gives atari at 1.

PROBLEM 167

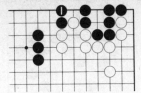

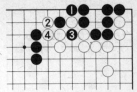

Correct Answer

Black 1 is a superb move that allows Black to link up his stones on the right with those on the left.

Wrong Answer

Taking a stone with 1 and 3 is answered by White 2 and 4. The black stones in the corner are now isolated and dead.

PROBLEM 168

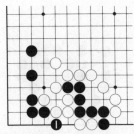

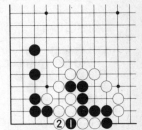

Correct Answer

Black 1 prevents White from rescuing his two stones in atari, so Black will be able to capture them on the next move.

Wrong Answer

Capturing immediately with 1 here lets White block at 2. Black can no longer link up, so his stones on the right are dead.

PROBLEM 169

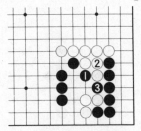

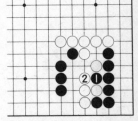

Correct Answer

Black 1 is the move that keeps the three white stones below separated from the ones above. These stones are now dead.

Wrong Answer

If Black plays 1, White secures a connection to his stones above with 2. Black has failed.

PROBLEM 170

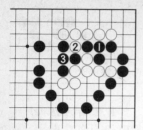

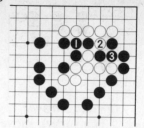

Correct Answer

Black 1 is the vital point. White 2 is answered by Black 3. White has no follow-up and so the seven white stones are dead.

Wrong Answer 1

If Black plays at 1, White gives atari with 2 and after Black 3 —

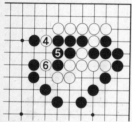

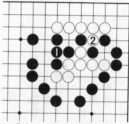

Continuation

White gives atari with 4 and 6, catching six black stones and rescuing his own seven stones in the process.

Wrong Answer 2

Black 1 here also fails. White gives double atari with 2 and it is now impossible to prevent White from linking up.

PROBLEM 171

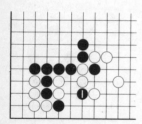

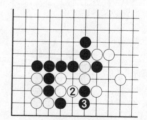

Correct Answer

Black 1 is the vital point. No matter how White plays, one of his two-stone groups will be captured.

For Reference 1

If White gives atari with 2, Black descends to 3 and White still can't prevent the capture of his two-stone group above.

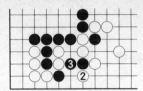

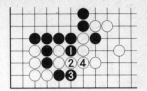

For Reference 2
If White 2, Black 3 catches the two white stones on the left. White can't connect because of a shortage of liberties.

Wrong Answer
Black 1 and 3 lead nowhere. After 4, White's bottom territory is impregnable.

PROBLEM 172

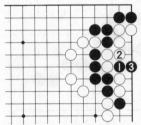

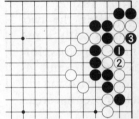

Correct Answer
Cutting with Black 1 is the vital point. If White exchanges 2 for 3, the six white stones above will die.

Wrong Answer
Black 1 and 3 will capture three white stones, but all the black stones below are dead.

PROBLEM 173

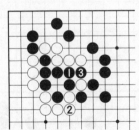

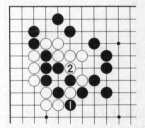

Correct Answer
Black 1 is the vital point. If White plays 2, Black captures at 3. Alternatively, if White 2 at 3, Black 3 at 2. Either way, the four pivotal black stones escape.

Wrong Answer
Capturing with Black 1 lets White take the vital point at 2. The four pivotal black stones are now unable to escape.

Correct Answer
Black 1 is the most profitable way to play. When White connects at 2, Black 3 secures the territory along the bottom.

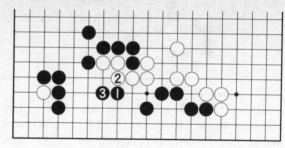

Wrong Answer
Going after the two white stones with 1 results in a big loss for Black. White 2 and 4 make a deep intrusion into Black's potential area.

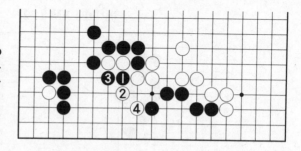

PROBLEM 175

Correct Answer
Taking the corner with Black 1 is the standard move in this position. Black's position is now absolutely secure.

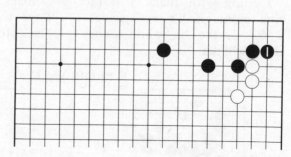

Wrong Answer
Black 1 here is overly defensive. After the exchange of 2 for 3, Black has suffered a big loss. Black 1 at A is also inferior to the correct answer.

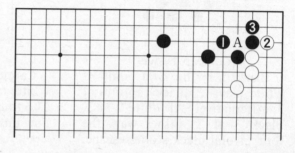

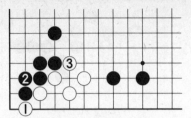

Correct Answer

White 1 may be a small point, but it is an essential move. When Black defends with 2, White stabilizes his position with 3.

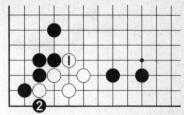

Wrong Answer

White 1 allows Black to play 2. White's stones now lack stability and can be easily attacked.

PROBLEM 177

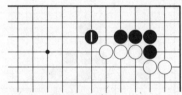

Correct Answer

Black must move out along the side by jumping to 1. He cannot let his stones be confined to the corner.

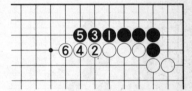

Wrong Answer

Black 1, 3 and 5 are too slow. Up to 6, White builds thickness in the center. Black's result is inferior to the correct answer.

PROBLEM 178

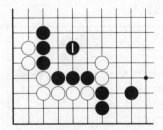

Correct Answer

Black 1 is the vital point for making good shape. Reinforcing weak points with moves like 1 is important.

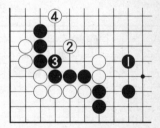

Wrong Answer

If Black neglects to reinforce his stones, White will attack with 2 and 4, putting Black's stones in great danger.

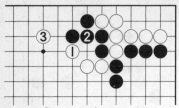 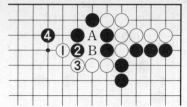

Correct Answer

White 1 threatens to capture two black stones in a snapback, so Black must connect at 2. After White 3, Black is almost captured.

Wrong Answer

White 1 lets Black easily escape with 2 and 4. Sacrificing a stone by playing 1 at A, and then giving atari at 2 after Black B, also lets Black escape.

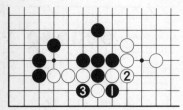 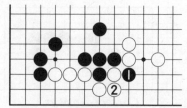

Correct Answer

Black 1 is the vital point. After White 2, Black 3 catches the four white stones on the left.

Wrong Answer

In response to Black 1, White connects at 2. Black has no follow-up, so Black 1 will be captured.

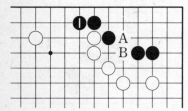 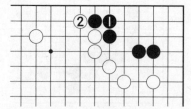

Correct Answer

Extending out to 1 is the correct move. If White next plays A, Black plays B. The territory at the top is firmly in Black's grasp.

Wrong Answer

Black 1 is overly defensive. White 2 confines Black to the corner. This result is vastly inferior to the correct answer.

PROBLEM 182

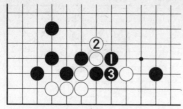

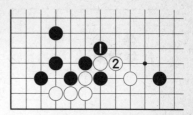

Correct Answer
Black should play at 1. If White 2, Black connects at 3. Black has an overwhelming advantage in this local situation. If White 2 at 3, Black takes at 2 for a good result.

Wrong Answer
If Black 1, White extends to 2, catching a black stone. White's position is intact. Black has failed.

PROBLEM 183

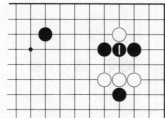

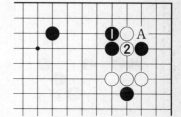

Correct Answer
Black 1 is the correct answer. Even if White can live in the corner, there is no other way but to connect against a peep.

Wrong Answer
Black 1 is bad. After White 2, the black stone in the corner is nearly dead. Black 1 at A is also answered by White 2. Again, Black's result is not good.

PROBLEM 184

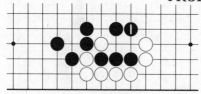

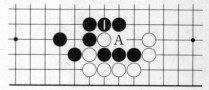

Correct Answer
In a position like this, making a 'bamboo joint' with 1 is the usual way to make sure the white stone doesn't escape.

Wrong Answer
Depending on the situation, Black 1 is also a possible move. However, Black 1 at A is almost always inferior.

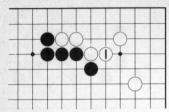 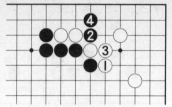

Correct Answer

Extending to White 1 is the standard response in this situation. It follows the proverb, "extend against a hane" (Black 1 in the problem diagram).

Wrong Answer

White 1 here is an overplay. White suffers a big loss when Black catches the two stones on the left with 2 and 4. White 1 at 2 is also an inferior move.

PROBLEM 186

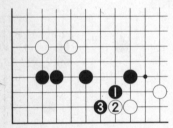 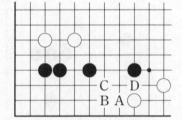

Correct Answer

Black 1 is the correct response. If White 2, Black stops White's intrusion with 3.

Wrong Answer

The responses from A to D are all inferior to the correct answer.

PROBLEM 187

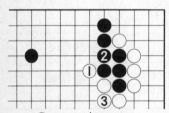 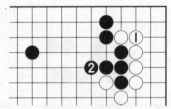

Correct Answer

Giving atari at 1 is the only move: it forces Black to make bad shape. Next, White connects solidly at 3.

Wrong Answer

White 1 lacks power. Black fixes up his shape with 2, forming territory at the top.

PROBLEM 188

Correct Answer
Even though White loses a stone, White has no choice but to link up along the bottom with 1.

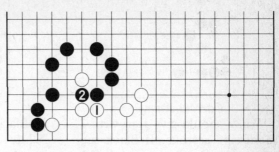

Wrong Answer
If White connects with 1, Black 2 and 4 cut his stones off from the outside. This is a big loss for White.

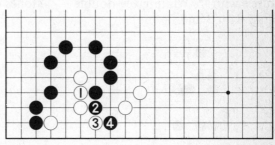

PROBLEM 189

Correct Answer
Black 1 is the right way to give atari. White's efforts to escape are futile as the sequence to Black 5 demonstrates.

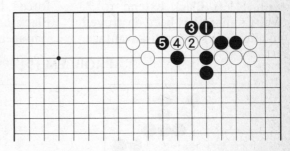

Wrong Answer
Black 1 and 3 throw away two stones for nothing. Black has suffered a big loss.

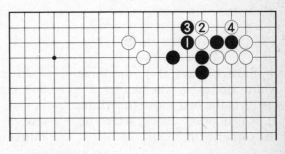

PROBLEM 190

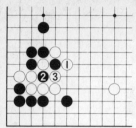

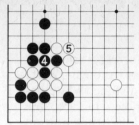

Correct Answer
White should give atari with 1, sacrificing a stone. If Black captures with 2, White gives double atari with 3 and —

Continuation
Black 4 is forced. Finally, White connects at 5, giving his stones excellent shape.

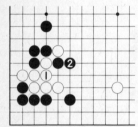

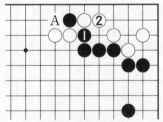

Wrong Answer
Defending against the atari with 1 lets Black extend to 2. White's shape has been destroyed and he's at a serious disadvantage.

Continuation
The sequence to Black 6 is forced, but there is no doubt that Black has ended up with an advantageous position.

PROBLEM 191

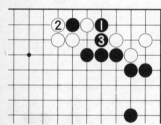

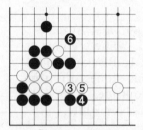

Correct Answer
If Black plays at 1, the three white stones in the corner are lost. 2 is the best move for White, at which point Black wraps up the corner with 3.

Wrong Answer
In response to Black 1, White will play 2 and all his stones are linked up. Expecting White to answer 1 at A is just wishful thinking.

PROBLEM 192

Correct Answer
White 1 is the correct response. If Black 2, White links up his two groups with 3.

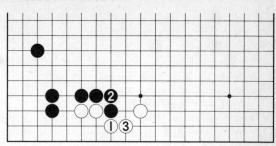

Wrong Answer
Cutting with White 1 is unreasonable. After Black 2 and 4, the two white stones to the left are dead and White's position is shattered.

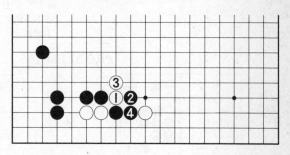

PROBLEM 193

Correct Answer
Invading with Black 1 is the correct answer. No matter how White plays after this it cannot be bad for Black.

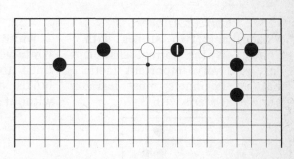

Wrong Answer
Black 1 is a bad move. White is helped to make the move he wants. An invasion is now impossible. It would have been better for Black not to have played here at all.

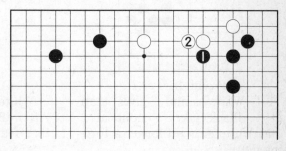

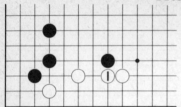

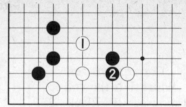

Correct Answer

There is only one way for White to play: link up his stones with 1.

Wrong Answer

Jumping out into the center with 1 lets Black play 2. White's position is now split into two groups, so he is at a disadvantage.

PROBLEM 195

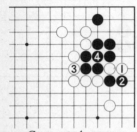

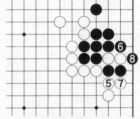

Correct Answer

Sacrificing two stones with White 1 is the correct answer. This is a very important tactic that all beginners must learn. White next ataris with 3 —

Continuation

White continues by squeezing White with 5 and 7. Black is confined to the corner and White builds a wall on the outside without any defects.

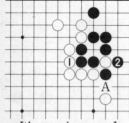

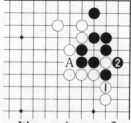

Wrong Answer 1

If White simply gives atari at 1, Black takes a stone at 2 and White A is no longer a forcing move.

Wrong Answer 2

White 1 here is also bad. After Black 2, White A loses its effect.

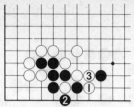

Correct Answer
Giving atari with White 1 is the vital point. After Black 2, White connects with 3, separating Black into two groups. Next —

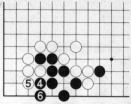

Continuation
Black must play 4 and 6 to live. With the black stone on the right isolated and weakened, White has made a big gain.

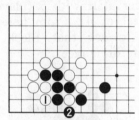

Wrong Answer 1
White 1 here is a mistake. After Black 2, it is impossible to separate the black stone on the right from the others.

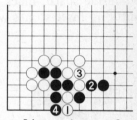

Wrong Answer 2
White 1 is also bad. Black gives atari with 2 and then gives another atari with 4. This is a big loss for White.

PROBLEM 197

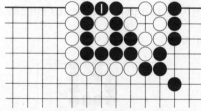

Correct Answer
Black can capture three stones altogether. First of all, Black takes two stones with 1. Next —

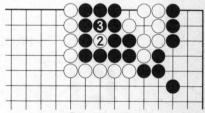

Continuation
To maintain the seki, White must play at 2, so Black can capture another stone with 3. It is usual to make these captures at the very end of the game.

PROBLEM 198

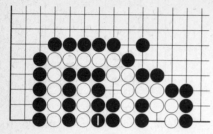

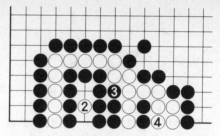

Correct Answer
The position is not a seki! Black's inside space is bigger than White's inside space. Black starts by capturing three stones with 1.

Continuation
If White 2, Black gives atari with 3 and after White 4, gives another atari with 5 (played to the left of 4). From here it is easy to see that Black wins the capturing race.

PROBLEM 199

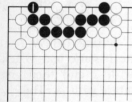

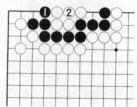

Correct Answer
Black 1 is the vital point for making life with a seki.

Wrong Answer
If Black gives atari to three stones with 1, White connects at 2, making a 5-point nakade, which is a dead shape for Black.

PROBLEM 200

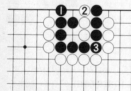

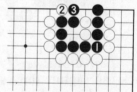

Correct Answer
Black 1 is the vital point. If White 2, Black 3 creates a seki.

Wrong Answer
Black 1 is a mistake. White exchanges 2 for 3 and Black cannot get a seki.

PROBLEM 201

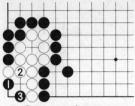

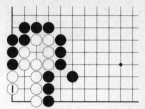

Correct Answer
Black 1 and 3 create a seki. White cannot attack the two black stones in the corner because of a shortage of liberties. Both sides are left with 0 points.

If White Plays First
If it were White's turn to play, he would play a move like 1 in the corner. His territory there is 5 points, so this move is worth 5 points.

PROBLEM 202

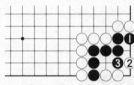

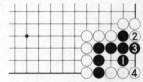

Correct Answer
Black 1 is the vital point. The sequence to Black 3 results in a seki. If White 2 at 3, Black plays 3 at 2 and it is still a seki.

Wrong Answer
If Black plays at 1, after 4 it is not a seki; it results in the death of the black group. White can make the 'bent four in the corner' shape by playing above 4.

PROBLEM 203

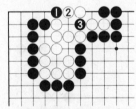

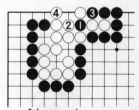

Correct Answer
Black must play 1 followed by 3. This order of moves is important. Because of a shortage of liberties, White cannot make two eyes.

Wrong Answer
If Black plays 1 first, White gets two eyes by playing 2 and 4. If Black 3 at 4, White 4 at 3 also gives him two eyes.

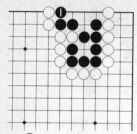

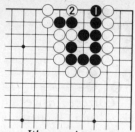

Correct Answer

Black 1 is the vital point. Black is now guaranteed of getting at least one eye at the top.

Wrong Answer

Black 1 lets White play at 2. It is now impossible for Black to get another eye at the top, so he is dead.

PROBLEM 205

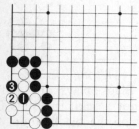

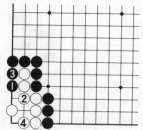

Correct Answer

Black 1 and 3 kill the white group.

Wrong Answer

Black 1 is a mistake. White is able to live with 2 and 4.

PROBLEM 206

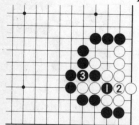

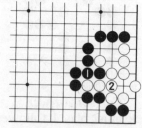

Correct Answer

Sacrificing a stone with 1 and then giving atari with 3 are the moves that kill the white group.

Wrong Answer

Giving atari with Black 1 lets White play at 2, giving him two eyes and life.

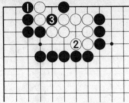

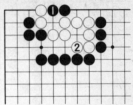

Correct Answer

Black 1 is the point of attack. If White tries to make an eye at 2, Black 3 catches two stones in a snapback, killing White in the process.

Wrong Answer

If Black 1, White 2. Or if Black 1 at 2, White 2 at 1. In either case, White is alive, so Black has failed.

PROBLEM 208

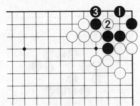

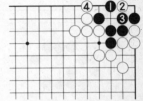

Correct Answer

Black 1 is the vital point. If White 2, Black descends to 3 and lives.

Wrong Answer

Black 1 here fails when White plays 2 and 4. Because of a shortage of liberties, Black cannot make a second eye.

PROBLEM 209

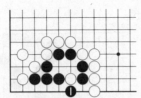

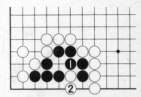

Correct Answer

Giving atari to the white stone from below gives Black two eyes and life.

Wrong Answer

Black 1, giving atari from above, fails. White descends to 2 and, because of a shortage of liberties, Black cannot block the escape of the two white stones.

PROBLEM 210

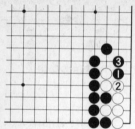

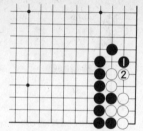

Correct Answer

Black 1 is the vital point of attack. If White 2, Black 3 leaves White without sufficient room to make two eyes.

Wrong Answer

Black 1 does not go deep enough. After 2, White has the space to make two eyes.

PROBLEM 211

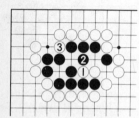

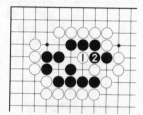

Correct Answer

White 1 is the vital point of attack. If Black 2, White 3 makes Black's second eye a false one, so Black is dead.

Wrong Answer

White 1 fails. After Black 2, White loses a stone, so Black gets two eyes and life.

PROBLEM 212

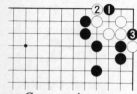

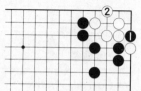

Correct Answer

Black 1 followed by 3 is the correct order of moves. White is dead.

Wrong Answer

Black 1 is a vital point, but it is not played in the proper order. White gets two eyes and life when he plays at 2.

PROBLEM 213

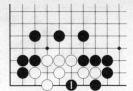

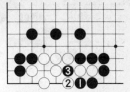

Correct Answer

Black 1 is the vital point for killing the white group. Since Black 1 cannot be separated from his other stones, White is left with only one eye.

Wrong Answer

If Black gives atari with 1, White sacrifices two stones with 2. After Black captures with 3, White retakes to the right of 3, leaving him with two eyes.

PROBLEM 214

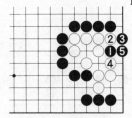

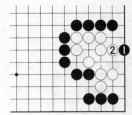

Correct Answer

Black 1 is the vital point for killing the white group. After the sequence to Black 5, the eye to the left of 4 becomes a false one, so White is dead.

Wrong Answer

Black 1 here fails. When White plays at 2, he gets two real eyes.

PROBLEM 215

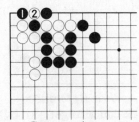

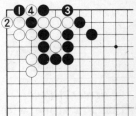

Correct Answer

Black 1 creates a ko. The life of the black and white stones at the top will be decided by this ko.

For Reference

If White plays at 2 in response to 1, Black plays at 3 and it is still a ko.

PROBLEM 216

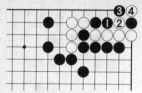

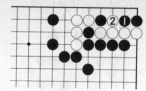

Correct Answer

If Black plays at 1, it becomes a ko with the sequence to White 4. The outcome of this ko determines the life or death of the white stones.

Wrong Answer

If Black plays at 1, the three black stones at the top right will be unconditionally captured after White 2.

PROBLEM 217

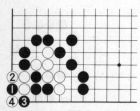

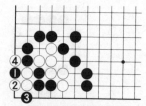

Correct Answer

Black 1 is the vital point for starting a ko. After White 4, the life of the white group will be decided by this ko.

Wrong Answer

Black 1 here fails. After White 4, the black stones at the bottom edge will be captured, allowing White to make two eyes.

PROBLEM 218

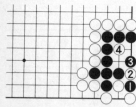

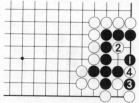

Correct Answer

Sacrificing a stone with 1 is the vital point for making a ko. White must destroy Black's eye shape with 4, so Black retakes the ko with 5 at 1. If Black wins this ko, his stones live.

For Reference

Black can also get a ko by playing at 1, but after White 4 he must look for a ko threat, so he has suffered a slight loss.

PROBLEM 219

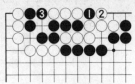

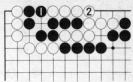

Correct Answer

Sacrificing a stone with Black 1 is a clever move. If White takes with 2, Black gives atari with 3 and wins the capturing race by one move.

Wrong Answer

If Black simply plays at 1, White connects at 2. It is now Black who loses the capturing race by one move.

PROBLEM 220

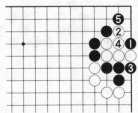

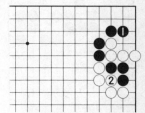

Correct Answer

Black 1 is the vital point. White struggles with 2 and 4, but after 5 it is clear that Black wins the capturing race by one move.

Wrong Answer

Black 1 is too slow. In a capturing race it is usually necessary to make contact plays. White plays at 2 and has three liberties to Black's two.

PROBLEM 221

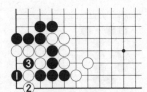

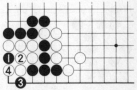

Correct Answer

Black 1 is the move. If White 2, Black catches White in a snapback with 3. If White 2 at 3, Black gives atari with 3 at 2.

Wrong Answer

Black 1 and 3 do not work. White answers with 2 and 4. Black loses the capturing race because White has an eye, while Black doesn't.

PROBLEM 222

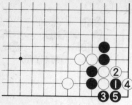

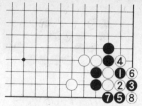

Correct Answer
Black is the correct answer. After the sequence to 5, it is easy to see that Black wins the capturing race by one move.

Wrong Answer
Black 1 and 3 do not work. The sequence to White 8 results in a ko.

PROBLEM 223

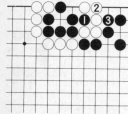

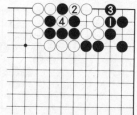

Correct Answer
Black 1 is the move. If White connects at 2, Black plays at 3 and White cannot attack the black stones to the left because of a shortage of liberties.

Wrong Answer
If Black plays at 1, White can destroy Black's eye with 2 and 4. The situation has become a ko, so Black has failed.

PROBLEM 224

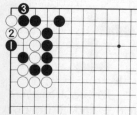

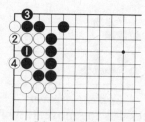

Correct Answer
Black 1 is a brilliant move. If White 2, Black 3 and Black wins the capturing race.

Wrong Answer
Giving atari with Black 1 fails. White plays 2 and 4 and wins the capturing race by one move.

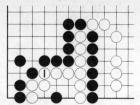

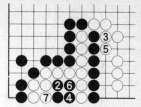

Correct Answer

White 1 is the vital point. White now wins the capturing race by one move as illustrated in the next two diagrams.

Continuation

From Black 2 to Black 6, both sides fill in the other's liberties. White then captures four stones with 7. Next —

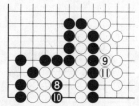

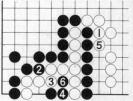

Continuation

The race continues, but after White 11 it is easy to see that Black loses the capturing race by one move.

Wrong Answer

If White starts to fill the outside liberties with 1, Black hits the vital point with 2. White now loses the capturing race by two moves.

PROBLEM 226

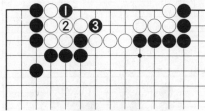

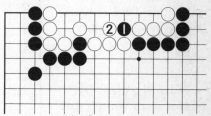

Correct Answer

Giving atari with Black 1 is the vital point. If White connects at 2, Black catches six stones with 3. Actually, White 2 should have been played at 3.

Wrong Answer

Black 1 has no follow-up move. White simply plays 2 and all his stones are safe.

Correct Answer 1
Giving atari with 1 is the vital point. If White connects at 2 (not the best move, as he should give up these stones), Black 3 will capture seven white stones.

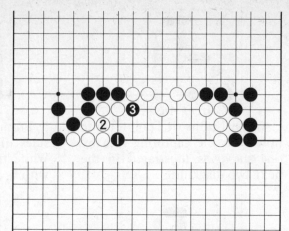

Correct Answer 2
Black 1 here will also capture the four white stones at the edge. If White 2, Black gives atari with 3 and White cannot defend because of a shortage of liberties.

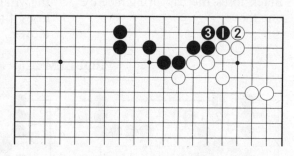

PROBLEM 228

Correct Answer
Black 1 and 3 are the endgame moves in this situation. For Black to play here first is worth more than ten points.

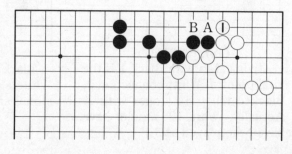

If White Plays First
If it were White's turn to play, either White 1 or the sequence White A – Black B – White 1 is correct. This gives White a profit of more than ten points.

PROBLEM 229

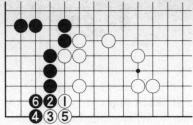

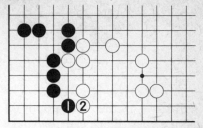

Correct Answer

White 1 is the best endgame move in this situation. After Black defends at 2, White 3 makes a further reduction in Black's territory while retaining sente.

If Black Plays First

If it were Black's turn, Black would also make a diagonal move, peeping into White's territory. In conclusion, whichever side gets to play first will make a big profit.

PROBLEM 230

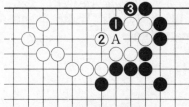

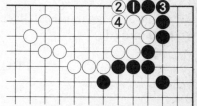

Correct Answer

Because White's three stones to the right are short of liberties, White 2 is the only response. If White 2 at 3, Black will play at A.

Wrong Answer

Black 1 and 3 are answered by White 2 and 4. This result is more than ten points worse for Black than the correct answer.

PROBLEM 231

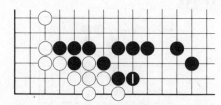

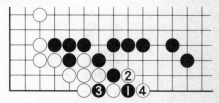

Correct Answer

There is no other move but Black 1. After this White can intrude no farther into Black's territory.

Wrong Answer

Black 1 is unreasonable. After White 2 and 4, Black can't defend his stones at 1 and 3, so White has devastated Black's territory.

PROBLEM 232

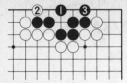

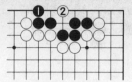

Correct Answer

Black 1 is the vital point for making eyes. Black can now make his second eye either at 3 or at 2.

Wrong Answer

If Black makes any other move, like 1, White kills him by taking the vital point of 2.

PROBLEM 233

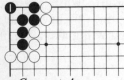

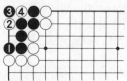

Correct Answer

Playing at 1 guarantees Black two eyes and life.

Wrong Answer

Black 1 fails. White 2 and 4 create a ko.

PROBLEM 234

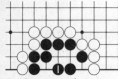

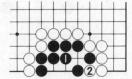

Correct Answer

Black 1 is the vital point for making two eyes and life.

Wrong Answer

Black 1 fails since White 2 destroys Black's second eye.

PROBLEM 235

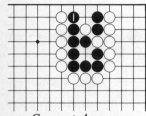

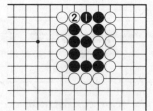

Correct Answer

Black 1 is the right way to stop the white stone from escaping. Black is now alive with two eyes.

Wrong Answer

Directly capturing with 1 fails. White 2 makes the eye below 1 a false one, so Black is dead.

PROBLEM 236

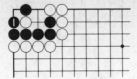

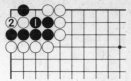

Correct Answer
Black 1 will capture a white stone and at the same time give Black life.

Wrong Answer
If Black gives atari at 1, White plays at 1 and reduces Black to one eye.

PROBLEM 237

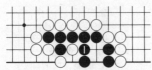

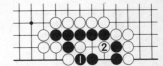

Correct Answer
Giving atari with Black 1 catches the white stone and gives Black two eyes.

Wrong Answer
If Black plays 1, after White 2 Black can't defend his two stones because of a shortage of liberties.

PROBLEM 238

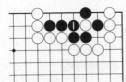

Correct Answer
Taking a stone with Black 1 gives Black two eyes and life.

Wrong Answer
If Black plays 1, White 2 and 4 destroy Black's eye on the right.

PROBLEM 239

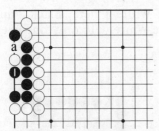

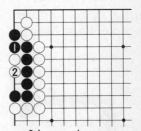

Correct Answer
1 gives Black two eyes. White at 'a' would be an illegal move.

Wrong Answer
Black 1 lets White play 2. Black is now reduced to one eye.

PROBLEM 240

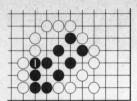

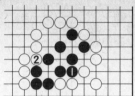

Correct Answer

If Black plays at 1, he will get his second eye two spaces to the right of 1.

Wrong Answer

If Black plays 1 here, White 2 will leave Black with one real eye and two false ones.

PROBLEM 241

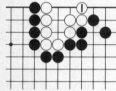

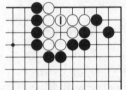

Correct Answer

1 gives White two eyes. No matter how Black attacks now, he cannot kill White

For Reference

White can also live with 1 here, but this move is at least two points less profitable.

PROBLEM 242

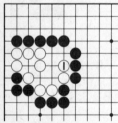

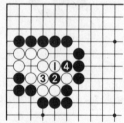

Correct Answer

White 1 makes another eye on the right, so White lives.

Wrong Answer

If White 1 here, Black 2 and 4 leave White with only one eye.

PROBLEM 243

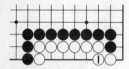

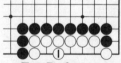

Correct Answer

White 1 guarantees that White will get two eyes.

For Reference

Compared to the correct answer, White 1 is worth a point less.

PROBLEM 244

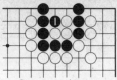

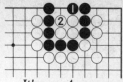

Correct Answer

Black 1 catches three stones and ensures that the final shape will become two eyes.

Wrong Answer

Black 1 is answered by White 2. Black is now left with a dead 4-point nakade shape.

PROBLEM 245

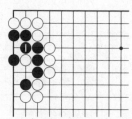

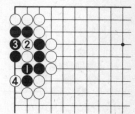

Correct Answer

Black 1 catches a white stone, giving Black two eyes and life.

Wrong Answer

If Black 1, White kills Black by playing 2 and 4.

PROBLEM 246

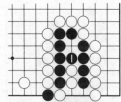

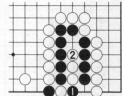

Correct Answer

Black 1 makes an eye above and also stops the two white stones below from escaping.

Wrong Answer

If Black directly captures with 1, White 2 makes a 3-point nakade shape, so Black is dead.

PROBLEM 247

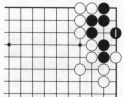

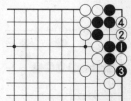

Correct Answer

Black 1 is a simple move which directly makes two eyes.

Wrong Answer

If Black plays 1, White 2 and 4 reduce Black to one eye.

PROBLEM 248

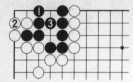

Correct Answer
Black 1 makes two eyes. If White 2, Black 3. If White 2 at 3, Black 3 at 2 catches two stones.

Wrong Answer
Giving atari with 1 destroys Black's only chance of making two eyes. Black is now dead.

PROBLEM 249

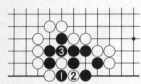

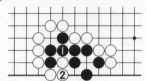

Correct Answer
If Black sacrifices a stone with 1, after 2, Black 3 traps two stones.

Wrong Answer
Black 1 is answered by White 2. Black has no follow-up move, so he is dead.

PROBLEM 250

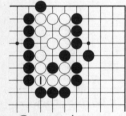

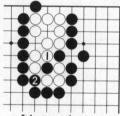

Correct Answer
White 1 makes an eye. The endangered black stone can't escape, so White lives unconditionally.

Wrong Answer
Capturing a stone with White 1 is answered by Black 2. White lives only if he can win the ko.

PROBLEM 251

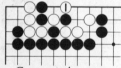

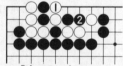

Correct Answer
White 1 is a superb move. Black can't capture because of a snapback, so White lives.

Wrong Answer
Capturing two stones directly with 1 fails. Black 2 catches two stones, so White dies.

PROBLEM 252

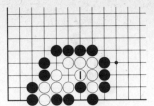

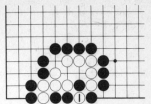

Correct Answer
White 1 makes it impossible for the three black stones to escape, so White gets two eyes.

Wrong Answer
White 1 results in the death of all the white stones when Black retakes to the left of 1 with 2.

PROBLEM 253

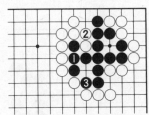

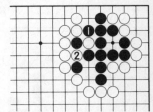

Correct Answer
If Black plays 1, he can make his second eye at either 2 or 3, depending on where White plays.

Wrong Answer
If Black captures a stone with 1, White 2 leaves Black with only one real eye, so Black is dead.

PROBLEM 254

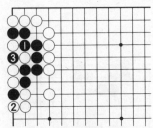

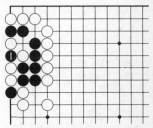

Correct Answer
If Black plays 1, he will capture two stones with 3, making two eyes.

Wrong Answer
Capturing two stones with 1 fails. White recaptures with 2, at the point below 1, leaving Black with a dead 4-point nakade shape.

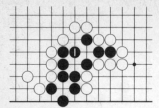

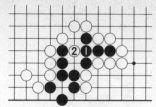

Correct Answer
Black 1 lets White captures two of his stones, but this secures the point below 1 as his second eye.

Wrong Answer
If Black connects at 1, White plays at 2. This stone can't be captured because of a shortage of liberties, so Black dies.

PROBLEM 256

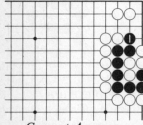

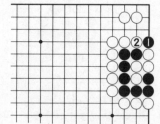

Correct Answer
Black must play 1 and not take the four white stones. After this move, if he then takes those stones, the resulting shape is a 4-point shape that lives.

Wrong Answer
If Black immediately takes with 1, after White 2, Black is left with a dead 3-point nakade shape.

PROBLEM 257

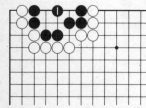

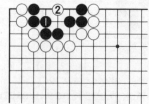

Correct Answer
Black 1 is the vital point for making eye shape. Black is now alive.

Wrong Answer
If Black plays any other point, his group dies. For example, if Black 1, White 2 kills Black.

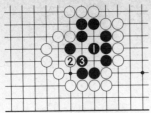 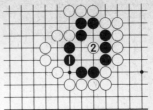

Correct Answer

Black 1 is the vital point for making eye shape. However White plays, Black will get two eyes.

Wrong Answer

Black 1 lets White make a 5-point nakade. After White plays 2, Black dies.

PROBLEM 259

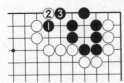 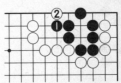

Correct Answer

1 makes room for Black's second eye, If White 2, Black 3 makes a second eye.

Wrong Answer

Black 1 is not wide enough. White plays 2 and Black can only get a false eye.

PROBLEM 260

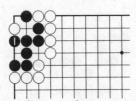 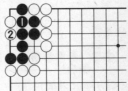

Correct Answer

Black 1 is the only move that gives Black two eyes and life.

Wrong Answer

If Black plays 1, White 2 kills the black stones.

PROBLEM 261

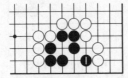 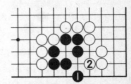

Correct Answer

1 gives Black the space he needs to make two eyes.

Wrong Answer

If Black 1, White 2 prevents Black from getting a second eye.

PROBLEM 262

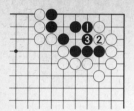

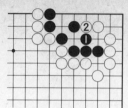

Correct Answer
Black 1 is the correct answer. Up to 3, Black gets two eyes.

Wrong Answer
If Black plays 1, White 2 makes Black's second eye false.

PROBLEM 263

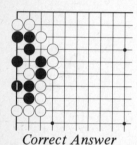

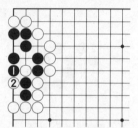

Correct Answer
Black 1 is a quiet move which guarantees two eyes for Black.

Wrong Answer
If Black gives atari with 1, White 2 gives Black a false eye.

PROBLEM 264

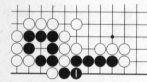

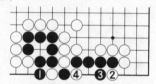

Correct Answer
Black 1 guarantees an eye on the right, so Black lives.

Wrong Answer
If Black takes with 1, White 2 and 4 destroy Black's second eye.

PROBLEM 265

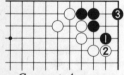

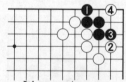

Correct Answer
Black 1 makes room for eyes in the corner. With 3, Black will easily get two eyes.

Wrong Answer
Black 1 is the wrong direction. White 2 and 4 kill the black group.

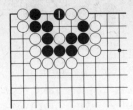

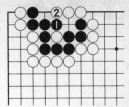

Correct Answer

Black 1 makes an eye to the left and ensures the capture of the lone white stone above, so Black gets two eyes and life.

Wrong Answer

If Black captures with 1, White 2 robs Black of his second eye, so his stones are dead.

PROBLEM 267

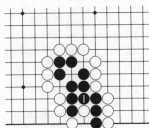

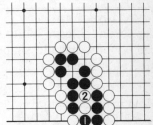

Correct Answer

Black secures the capture of a white stone, so Black gets his second eye at the bottom.

Wrong Answer

Black 1 just puts himself into atari. White captures four stones with 2, so all the black stones are dead.

PROBLEM 268

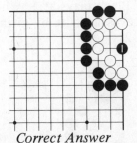

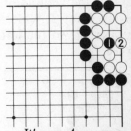

Correct Answer

Black 1 is the vital point of the 5-point nakade shape. White cannot make two eyes and so he is dead.

Wrong Answer

Any other move, like Black 1 here, would allow White to live with two eyes.

PROBLEM 269

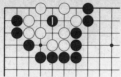 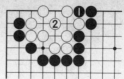

Correct Answer

Black 1 is the vital point of the 5-point nakade shape. White dies.

Wrong Answer

1 lets White take the vital point of 2, giving him two eyes.

PROBLEM 270

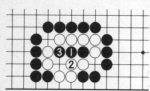 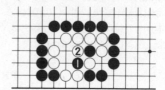

Correct Answer

Black 1 and 3 leave White with a dead 3-point nakade shape. If White 2 at 3, Black 3 at 2.

Wrong Answer

If Black gives atari with 1, White easily lives after he captures with 2.

PROBLEM 271

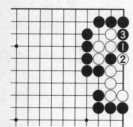 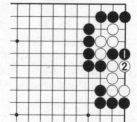

Correct Answer

Black 1 is the vital point. After exchanging 2 for 3, White is left with a false eye to the left of 2.

Wrong Answer

If Black plays at 1, White gets two eyes and life by giving atari with 2.

PROBLEM 272

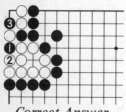 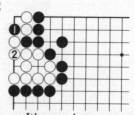

Correct Answer

If Black sacrifices with 1 and 3, all the white stones will die.

Wrong Answer

The order is important. If Black 1 first, White gets two eyes with 2.

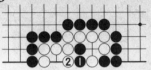

Correct Answer

Black 1 is the vital point. Black will eventually be reduced to a dead 3-point nakade shape.

Wrong Answer

If Black 1, White 2 captures two stones, getting two eyes and life.

PROBLEM 274

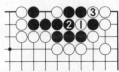

Correct Answer

White sacrifices a stones with 1 and then destroys Black's eye on the right with 3.

Wrong Answer

Without the sacrifice, White 1 fails. Black 2 gives Black two real eyes.

PROBLEM 275

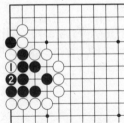

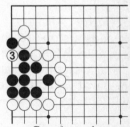

Correct Answer

White adds a stone to the one already in atari. After Black 2 —

Continuation

White sacrifices another stone with 3, giving Black a false eye.

PROBLEM 276

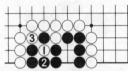

Correct Answer

White sacrifices a stone with 1, followed by Black 3. If Black 2 at 3, White 3 at 2, capturing four stones.

Wrong Answer

Without the sacrifice, White 1 lets Black get two eyes with 2.

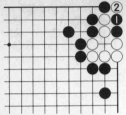

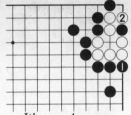

Correct Answer

Black sacrifices two stones with 1. After White 2, Black retakes at the point 1 with 3. White is left with only one eye.

Wrong Answer

Black 1 lets White capture with 2, leaving him with two perfect eyes.

PROBLEM 278

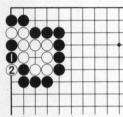

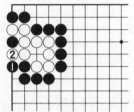

Correct Answer

Black adds a stone to the one already in atari. When White takes with 2, Black sacrifices again by throwing in at 1 with 3, leaving White with a false eye.

Wrong Answer

If Black plays at 1, White gets two perfect eyes when he captures at 2.

PROBLEM 279

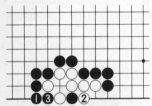

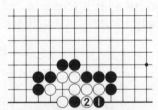

Correct Answer

Black 1 is the correct answer. White can't play at 3 because of a shortage of liberties. When White takes with 2, Black 3 leaves White with only one real eye.

Wrong Answer

If Black plays at 1, 2 gives White two perfect eyes and life.

PROBLEM 280

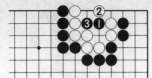

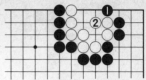

Correct Answer

Black 1 is the vital point of life and death. If White 2, after 3, White eventually will be reduced to a dead 3-point nakade shape.

Wrong Answer

Black 1 is bad because it provokes White to play 2. White now has two eyes and can't be killed.

PROBLEM 281

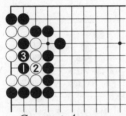

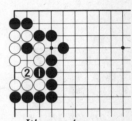

Correct Answer

Black 1 and 3 are the correct moves. White is now reduced to a dead 3-point nakade shape.

Wrong Answer

Black 1 helps White make two eyes. The only way to kill White is to sacrifice three stones.

PROBLEM 282

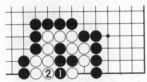

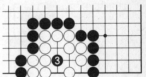

Correct Answer

Black 1 gives White a dead 4-point nakade shape. After 2, —

Continuation

Black plays 3 in the middle of the nakade shape and White will eventually be reduced to one eye.

PROBLEM 283

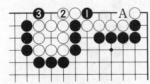

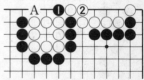

Correct Answer

Black 1 or A will kill White. If White 2, Black 3 destroys the second eye on the edge.

Wrong Answer

Black 1 or A fails. After 2, White can make another eye on the right.

PROBLEM 284

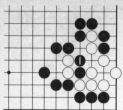

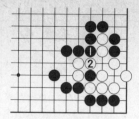

Correct Answer

Black 1 catches the two white stones to the left. White is dead.

Wrong Answer

Giving atari with Black 1 is answered by 2. White gets two eyes.

PROBLEM 285

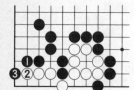

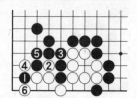

Correct Answer

Black 1 and 3 prevent White from getting a second eye at the bottom, so he is dead.

Wrong Answer

Black 1 is an overplay. After a series of ataris to 6, White secures life for his group.

PROBLEM 286

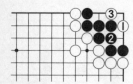

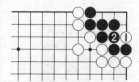

Correct Answer

White 1 and 3 create a dead bent-four-in-the-corner shape.

Wrong Answer

Giving atari with 1 fails. After White 2, Black has no follow-up.

PROBLEM 287

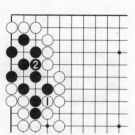

Correct Answer

If White 1, all Black's eyes except the one on the edge are false.

Wrong Answer

If White gives atari with 1, Black 2 results in three eyes!

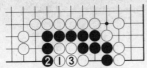

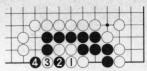

Correct Answer

White 1 and 3 give Black a dead 5-point nakade shape.

Wrong Answer

If White 1, Black 2 and 4 result in a ko. White has failed.

PROBLEM 289

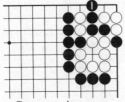

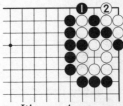

Correct Answer

1 is a superb move. Because of a shortage of liberties, White can't make an eye in the corner.

Wrong Answer

If Black captures with 1, White gets his second eye in the corner by playing at 2.

PROBLEM 290

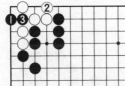

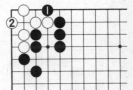

Correct Answer

Black 1 is the vital point. If 2, Black 3 finishes off White.

Wrong Answer

Black 1 lets White get two eyes in the corner with 2.

PROBLEM 291

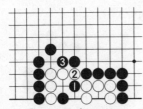

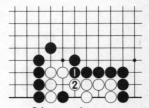

Correct Answer

Black 1 is a superb move. After 3, White can't give atari to the black stones, so he dies.

Wrong Answer

If Black 1, White 2 catches the lone black stone, so White is absolutely alive.

PROBLEM 292

Correct Answer
Black 1 and 3 kill White. If he now attacks the black stones, he puts himself into atari.

Wrong Answer
Black 1 is answered by White 2. No matter how Black plays next, White will get two eyes.

PROBLEM 293

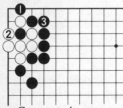

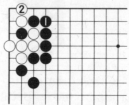

Correct Answer
Black gives atari with 1 and then defends with 3. White has only one eye.

Wrong Answer
Defending at 1 lets White play 2, giving him two eyes and life.

PROBLEM 294

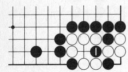

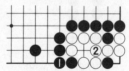

Correct Answer
Black 1 kills all the white stones. There is no way White can get out of atari.

Wrong Answer
If Black connects at 1, 2 gives White two eyes and life.

PROBLEM 295

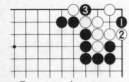

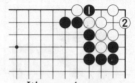

Correct Answer
Black 1 is the vital point for eye shape. After Black 3, White has only one eye.

Wrong Answer
Playing 1 first is the wrong order of moves. White makes two perfect eyes with 2.

PROBLEM 296

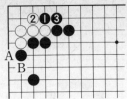

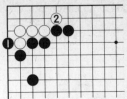

Correct Answer

If Black 1 and 3, White doesn't have room in the corner for two eyes. If White A, Black B.

Wrong Answer

Black 1 is in the wrong direction. White can't be killed after 2.

PROBLEM 297

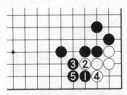

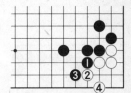

Correct Answer

Black 1 is the vital point. After Black 5, White can't get two eyes.

Wrong Answer

Black 1 and 3 are slack. White gets two eyes with 2 and 4.

PROBLEM 298

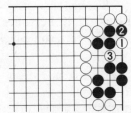

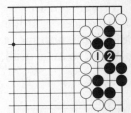

Correct Answer

White 1 is the vital point. If 2, White 3 leaves Black with one eye.

Wrong Answer

If White plays 1, Black will get his second eye to the right of 2.

PROBLEM 299

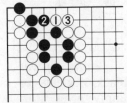

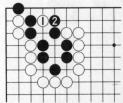

Correct Answer

White 1 makes the black eye at the top a false one. Black dies.

Wrong Answer

If White 1, Black 2 catches this stone, giving Black another eye.

PROBLEM 300

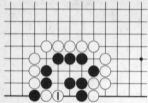

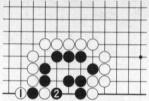

Correct Answer
White 1 is the vital point. Black cannot make two eyes no matter how he plays.

Wrong Answer
If White takes at 1, Black easily gets two eyes and lives by playing at 2.

PROBLEM 301

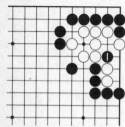

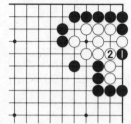

Correct Answer
Black sacrifices a stone at 1. This point will become a false eye for White, so he is dead.

Wrong Answer
If Black 1, it becomes a ko after White 2, so Black has failed.

PROBLEM 302

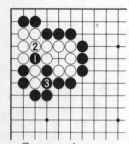

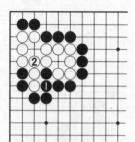

Correct Answer
Black sacrifices a stone with 1. If White 2, Black gives atari with 3 and White is reduced to only one eye.

Wrong Answer
If Black neglects to sacrifice and simply gives atari with 1, Black connects at 2 and gets two perfect eyes.

PROBLEM 303

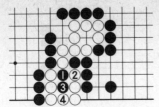

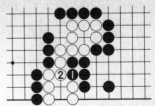

Correct Answer

First of all Black sacrifices two stones with 1 and 3, then, when White takes with 4, throws in a stone at the point 1 with 5. Black is reduced to one eye.

Wrong Answer

If Black plays 1, White easily lives by playing at 2.

PROBLEM 304

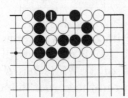

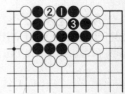

Correct Answer

Black 1 creates a seki. If White sacrifices four stones, Black will live with two eyes.

Wrong Answer

In response to Black 1, White gives atari with 2. Now after Black takes with 3, he is left with a dead 4-point nakade shape.

PROBLEM 305

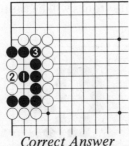

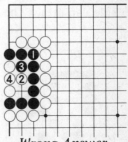

Correct Answer

Black 1 threatens to get two eyes, so White must connect at 2. Next Black plays 3 and the result is a seki.

Wrong Answer

If Black plays 1 first, White plays 2. Now after the exchange of 3 for 4, Black will be left with a dead 4-point nakade shape.

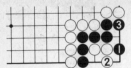
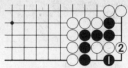

Correct Answer

Black 1 and 3 create a seki. If White 2 at 3, Black plays 3 at 2 and lives without seki.

Wrong Answer

If Black 1, White plays at 2 and the black stones are dead.

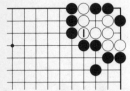
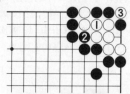

Correct Answer

White 1 creates a seki with the three black stones in the corner.

Wrong Answer

If White takes two stones with 1 and 3, Black retakes with 4 to the left of 3. White has a dead bent-four-in-the-corner shape.

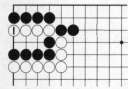
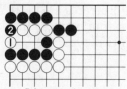

Correct Answer

A seki results if White plays 1. Neither side can attack the other.

Wrong Answer

If White 1, Black plays 2 and the white stones will be captured.

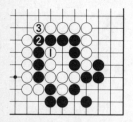
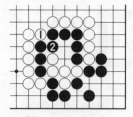

Correct Answer

White 1 and 3 create a seki between the nine black and six white stones.

Wrong Answer

Giving atari with White 1 results in the capture of five white stones when Black plays 2.

PROBLEM 310

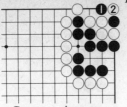

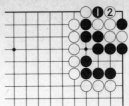

Correct Answer

After Black 1, White has no choice but to fight a ko with 2 if he is to kill Black.

Wrong Answer

Black 1 lets White save his corner stones, so all of Black's stones will die.

PROBLEM 311

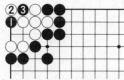

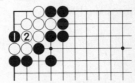

Correct Answer

Black 1 is the vital point for starting a ko. White 2 is forced and the ko begins with Black 3.

Wrong Answer

Giving atari with 1 is answered by White 2. White now lives unconditionally.

PROBLEM 312

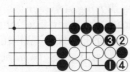

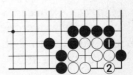

Correct Answer

Black starts a ko with the sequence to White 4.

Wrong Answer

If Black plays 1, White gets two perfect eyes by playing at 2.

PROBLEM 313

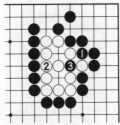

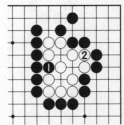

Correct Answer

Black 1 and 3 start a ko for the life of death of White's group.

Wrong Answer

If Black 1, White gets two perfect eyes when he plays at 2.

PROBLEM 314

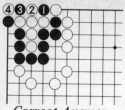 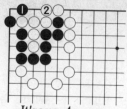

Correct Answer

Black makes two sacrifices with 1 and 3. The order of moves is important. The ko begins when White takes with 4.

Wrong Answer

If Black plays 1 first, White connects at 2. Black has no follow-up move, so all his stones die.

PROBLEM 315

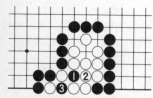 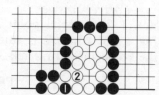

Correct Answer

If Black sacrifices a stone at 1, after White takes with 2, he can get a ko by capturing at 3.

Wrong Answer

Without the sacrifice, there is no ko. After Black 1, White connects at 2 and gets two perfect eyes.

PROBLEM 316

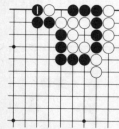 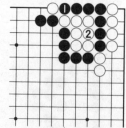

Correct Answer

Black 1 is a superb move. White cannot make a move to defend himself because of a shortage of liberties.

Wrong Answer

Black just puts himself into atari when he plays at 1, so White captures seven stones with 2.

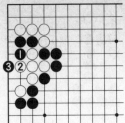

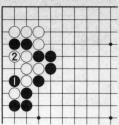

Correct Answer

By playing at 1, Black increases his own liberties by one and reduces White's by one. If White 2, Black gives atari with 3 and wins the capturing race by one move.

Wrong Answer

Giving atari with Black 1 results in the loss of Black's two stones at the top, so Black has failed.

PROBLEM 318

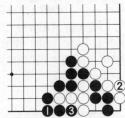

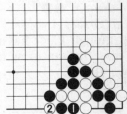

Correct Answer

Black can win the capturing race by one move if he connects at 1 and then gives atari with 3.

Wrong Answer

Black 1 just throws away two stones. In addition, the four black stones in the corner are lost.

PROBLEM 319

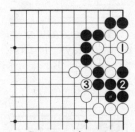

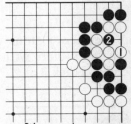

Correct Answer

If White makes an eye with 1, there is no way that Black can win the capturing race. After White 3, Black can't make a move without putting himself into atari.

Wrong Answer

White 1 is not the way to make an eye. Black 2 puts seven white stones into atari, so Black's six stones are safe.

PROBLEM 320

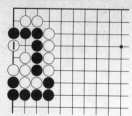

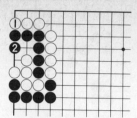

Correct Answer
If White makes an eye with 1, the six black stones above will die.

Wrong Answer
If White plays 1 from above, the situation will become a seki.

PROBLEM 321

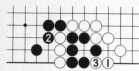

Correct Answer
Even though Black has an eye, White wins the capturing race by playing 1 and 3.

Wrong Answer
White 1 here fails. Black wins the capturing race by one move.

PROBLEM 322

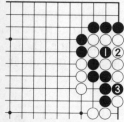

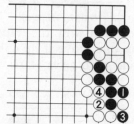

Correct Answer
Black sacrifices a stone with 1 and then gives atari with 3. If White 2 at 3, Black 3 at 2.

Wrong Answer
If Black plays 1 first, after White 2 and 4, Black can't get out of atari.

PROBLEM 323

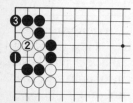

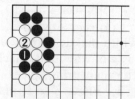

Correct Answer
Black 1 forces White to play 2. After 3, Black catches five stones.

Wrong Answer
If Black 1, Black's three stones below will be captured by White.

PROBLEM 324

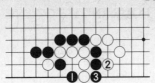

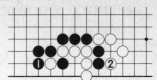

Correct Answer
Black 1 is the move that kills the six white stones. If White 2, Black gives atari with 3.

Wrong Answer
Giving atari to one white stone fails. White plays 2 and catches two black stones.

PROBLEM 325

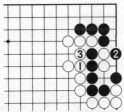

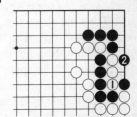

Correct Answer
Playing 1 and 3 in any order catches the five black stones.

Wrong Answer
If White 1, Black 2 sets up a snapback for the three white stones.

PROBLEM 326

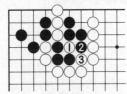

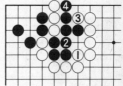

Correct Answer
If White sacrifices a stone with 1 and then gives atari with 3, he wins the capturing race by one move.

Wrong Answer
Without the sacrifice, it is Black who wins the capturing race.

PROBLEM 327

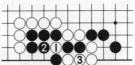

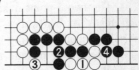

Correct Answer
Black sacrifices a stone with 1 and then gives atari with 3. In this way he will capture eight stones.

Wrong Answer
If White immediately gives atari with 1, he loses the capturing race by one move.

APPENDIX: NAKADE AND BENT FOUR IN THE CORNER

Nakade

It often happens that after you take the trouble to capture some stones, thinking that you've made eye shape, your opponent plays back inside this area and your group is reduced to one eye. This situation is known as 'nakade'. In the following, we will explain the basics of life and death of the various nakade positions.

Dia. 1. These are the two basic shapes of the 3-point nakade. In both positions, A is the vital point. If Black can play at A first, White will die. However, White gets two perfect eyes and life if he can play at A.

Dia. 2. There are three basic 4-point nakade shapes which can be killed. In the position at the bottom, A is the vital point. The life or death of the white group will be decided by whichever side gets to play this point.

In the position at the upper left, White is dead as he stands. If White plays inside his own nakade, he reduces himself to a dead 3-point nakade shape.

The 4-point nakade in the upper right corner is a special case. If White does not have more than one liberty on the outside, Black can start a ko for the life of the white group. Otherwise, White is unconditionally alive. (See Problem 15 on page 6.)

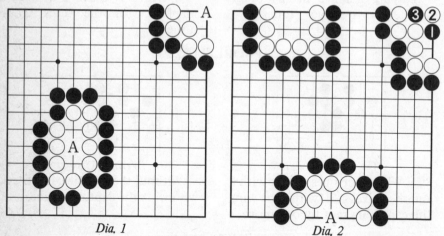

Dia. 1   Dia. 2

Dia. 3. The two 5-point nakade shapes shown here are the only ones that can be killed. If Black A, White dies. If White gets to play at A first, he lives. All other 5-point nakade shapes are, in principle, alive.

Dia. 4. The largest nakade that can be killed is a 6-point nakade. The 6-point nakade shown at the top of this diagram is known as 'flower six'. If Black plays at A, White will be reduced to one eye.

The rectangular 6-point nakade in the corner can be killed only if all the liberties on the outside are filled.

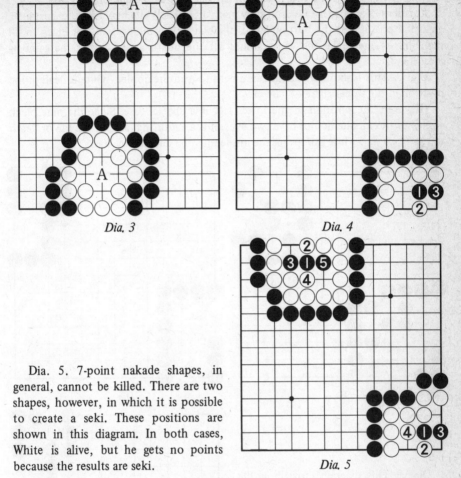

Dia. 3

Dia. 4

Dia. 5. 7-point nakade shapes, in general, cannot be killed. There are two shapes, however, in which it is possible to create a seki. These positions are shown in this diagram. In both cases, White is alive, but he gets no points because the results are seki.

Dia. 5

In summary, it is possible to kill stones making up 3-point nakade shapes to 6-point nakade shapes. 3-point nakades are the simplest to understand; the other shapes often present problems as to whether or not they are alive. Therefore, it is important that you familiarize yourself with these shapes, so that you can instantaneously determine the life-and-death status of these stones when confronted with them in a game.

Bent Four in the Corner

The Japanese rules of go are, for the most part, very easy to understand, but there is one rule in which confusion often arises. This is the shape known as 'bent four in the corner'.

Dia. 1. In the position in the upper right corner, White has the bent-four-in-the-corner shape. According to the rules, White's stones are unconditionally dead and they can be taken off the board without further play at the end of the game.

Furthermore, it doesn't matter how many liberties White may have, for instance, as in the position at the bottom left of the board. It is unnecessary for Black to fill them in: he may take the white stones off the board at the end of the game as they stand.

Dia. 2. This is another example of a bent four in the corner. White is dead in the position in the upper right.

However, the position in the lower left is a special case. Since the nine black stones in the middle do not have two eyes, it is a capturing race, so the life or death of the black and white groups on the inside must be decided by a ko.

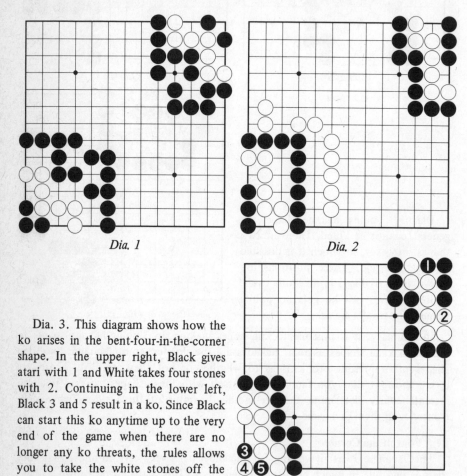

Dia. 1   Dia. 2

Dia. 3. This diagram shows how the ko arises in the bent-four-in-the-corner shape. In the upper right, Black gives atari with 1 and White takes four stones with 2. Continuing in the lower left, Black 3 and 5 result in a ko. Since Black can start this ko anytime up to the very end of the game when there are no longer any ko threats, the rules allows you to take the white stones off the board without playing out this ko.

Dia. 3

GO ASSOCIATIONS

The following is a list of national go associations throughout the world. If you have trouble locating other go players in your community, your local go organization may be able to help you.

ARGENTINA
Argentina Go Association
c/o Mr. Guillermo E. Zucal
Aroz 2730 -6o,
1425 Capital Federal
Tel. 71-3182

AUSTRALIA
Australian Go Association,
c/o Bill Leveritt,
"Denmora",
20 Cowlishaw Street,
Bowen Hills, QLD, 4006

AUSTRIA
Osterreichischer Go-Verband,
c/o Dr. Alfred Kriegler,
1030 Wien,
Rechte Bahngasse 28/2,
Tel. 7238335

BRAZIL
Brazil Ki-in
c/o Mr. Toshikatsu Takamori,
Rua Maria Figueiredo,
350 Sao Paulo,
Tel. 289-4062

CANADA
Canadian Go Association,
c/o Mr. Tibor Bognar,
8982 St. Hubert,
Montreal, Quebec H2M 1Y6
Tel. 387-1646

CHINA
China Weiqi Association,
Ti-yu-guan Lu 9,
Peking, Tel. 753110

CZECHOSLOVAKIA
Czechoslovak Go Association,
c/o Dr. Dusan Prokop,
Laubova 8,
130-00 Praha 3, CSSR
Tel. 276565

DENMARK
Denmark Go Association,
c/o Mr. Frank Hansen,
Nordre Frihavnsgade 24,
2100 Copenhagen,
Tel. 01-269460

FINLAND
Finland Go Association,
c/o Mr. Keijo Alho,
Kuusitie 8 A 14,
00270 Helsinki 27,
Tel. 90-483401

FRANCE
Federation Francaise de Go,
B.P. 9506,
75262 Paris Cedex 06

F. R. GERMANY
Deutscher Go Bund,
c/o Mr. Martin Stiassny,
Am Burgturm 2,
D-4048 Grevenbroich I,
Tel. 02181-42021

HONG KONG
Hong Kong Go Club,
458 Nathan Road,
8th Floor, B Flat,
Kowloon,
Tel. 3-857728

HUNGARY
Hungary Go Association,
c/o Mr. Gacs Istvan,
H-1085 Budapest,
Saletrom 6

ITALY
Italian Go Association,
c/o Raffaele Rinaldi,
Via La Marmora 18,
Milano,
Tel. 02-581523

JAPAN
    Nihon Ki-in,
    7-2 Gobancho,
    Chiyoda-ku, Tokyo 102,
    Tel. 03-262-6161

KOREA
    Korea Baduk Association,
    13-4. Kwanchul-Dong,
    Chongro-gu, Seoul,
    Tel. 723-0150

MEXICO
    Mexican Go Association,
    c/o Mr. Carlos Torres,
    Watteau 15-2, Col. Nonoalco,
    Delegacion Benito Juarez 03720
    Tel. 563-2302

NETHERLANDS
    Dutch Go Association,
    c/o Mr. J. H. van Frankenhuysen,
    J. Verhulststraat 125,
    1071 NA Amsterdam
    Tel. 020-739232

NEW ZEALAND
    National Seretary, N. Z. Go Society,
    c/o Mr. Peter Rochford,
    Victoria University, Private Bag,
    Wellington
    Tel. (Home) 727267

NORWAY
    Norwegian Go Association,
    c/o Mr. Morten Skogen,
    Kzempeveien 13E,
    N-4600 Kristiansand Syd,
    Tel. 42-91373

POLAND
    Warsaw Go Club,
    c/o Mr. Leszek Dziumowicz,
    Nowy Swiat 47/3a,
    P00-042 Warszawa

RUMANIA
    c/o Mr. Gheorghe Paun,
    Institute of Mathematics Str.,
    Academiei 14,
    70109 Bucuresti
    Tel. (Home) 256754

SINGAPORE
    Singapore Go Association,
    c/o Mr. Gin Hor Chan,
    Dept. of Mathematics,
    National University of Singapore
    Kent Ridge, Singapore 0511,
    Tel. 7756666, Ext. 2083

SPAIN
    Spanish Go Association,
    c/o Mr. Ambrosio Wang An-Po,
    Vallehermoso 89,
    Madrid

SWEDEN
    The Swedish Go Association,
    c/o Mr. Per-Inge Olsson,
    Safirgangen 24,
    S-13 549 Tyreso,
    Tel. 08-770-0927

SWITZERLAND
    Swiss Go Federation,
    c/o Mr. Tamotsu Takase,
    20 Ch. des Grangettes,
    1224 Chene-bougerie, Geneve,
    Tel. 489541

TAIWAN
    Chinese Taipei Wei-ch'i Association,
    c/o Mr. C. S. Shen,
    4th Fl., Kuang Fu Building,
    No. 35 Kuang Fu S. Rd.,
    Taipei, Taiwan R. O. C.
    Tel. 7614117

UNITED KINGDOM
    British Go Association,
    c/o Mr. Norman R. Tobin,
    10 West Common Road,
    Uxbridge, Middlesex UB8 1NZ,
    Tel. 0895-30511

USA
    American Go Association
    P. O. Box 397,
    Old Chelsea Station,
    New York, N. Y. 10011

YUGOSLAVIA
    Go Savez Jugoslavije,
    c/o Mr. Peter Gaspari,
    Aleseva 3, 61210 Ljubljana –
    Sentvid. Tel. (061) 52-111